EAST GERMANY

and the

ESCAPE

Kitchen Table Memoirs

For
Christine:
May you enjoy the
many adventures!
Best Wishes,
Doris Kienitz

BY DORIS KIENITZ

Editor: George Down of *The Corporate Word*
Photo of Doris Kienitz: Jerri Whiting
Photo of Alfred Kientiz: Doris Kienitz

Published by:

FriesenPress
Suite 300 – 852 Fort Street
Victoria, BC, Canada V8W 1H8

www.friesenpress.com

Distributed to the trade by The Ingram Book Company

Table of Contents

Dedication

This book is dedicated to my half-German children: Michelle, Alexander and Philipp – be the best you can be, speak truthfully, love passionately, live freely and joyously; don't assume or take anything personally, and above all practise loving-kindness to everyone. And always remember your heritage.

Introduction

My father, Alfred Kienitz (called Fred now in Canada by his friends), has a knack for telling stories. But they're not fiction – these events actually happened. And each time he tells a story, it's told exactly the same as the last time he told it, usually sitting around the supper table.

The stories always seemed to flow. To me, as a young child, it would be somewhat interesting, but unimaginable. As a teen, it would be: "Oh my God, not another one of his stories!" – one of those we've heard over and over again.

As an adult one begins to appreciate the tales about the war – the fact that most people were so poor, and all the hard work they endured when they were supposed to be enjoying their childhood. This was a time in their lives that was robbed of them in the name of survival. In most of our societies we know nothing of what they experienced during war or depression, or what life was like back in the 'old country'.

Because this information is now so scarce and so valuable I decided to write down the events that had been shared with me so many times before. Dad's memory for dates, places, names and events is incredible. It certainly is a gift. He can remember the last names of all of his neighbours where he lived while growing up! Sometimes I would ask him a question during the writing of the book, as I had forgotten the details, and when he verified the facts in the story it would be exactly as he had told it the first time. If he did not know the answer, he would simply say he didn't remember. Keep in mind that most of these events took place over 50 years ago! My only regret is that we did not finish this sooner, while my mom was still alive. She could have contributed her stories as well. I'm able to recount a few from my memory bank, and her younger sister helped fill in the holes. We actually began writing this book when Mom was still with us. After she passed away in January of 2006, I took a long hiatus before I was able to resume where we left off.

Now I have to tell you about my mother. She was the nicest, sweetest, kindest, most unselfish person. She worked hard all her life, and her painful hands, crooked fingers and poor health in later life proved it. She seldom complained even though many times pain filled her body. Baking, cooking and needlework were a few of her many passions. Her cooking was delicious, her baking scrumptious, including the most wonderful German Torten (fancy layered cakes). She loved her free-range chickens and cared for them almost to the very end of her life. Customers raved about the yellow yolk and delicious flavour. I miss her dearly, and am so grateful for my time with her.

I am doubly grateful that Dad is still with us, that he is able to chronicle this small part of some history in a very thought-provoking way. There were many events that took place especially when he was around the age of fourteen and fifteen. The what ifs are incredible. So many instances could have turned out much worse ending in death or imprisonment. I am so thankful for his bravery and determination, otherwise, we his children and future generations would not be here to experience life as we know it.

My writing of this book was extremely hard on Dad. He cried often while recounting stories of his painful adolescence. Once a week or more we persevered through tears and sad memories, and after a few hours, we would call it quits for another day. But there were many laughs along the way as well. Dad and his brothers, especially Gustav, were jokesters.

In conversation with my Uncle Gustav one day, a fascinating story came to light, about how he raised $30,000 in a few weeks while still living at home in East Germany. I felt compelled to add this to the collection of East Germany stories. Once you've read it I'm sure you'll understand why.

Being German, Dad may be known to some as 'the enemy', even though he neither fought nor cared to fight in the war. As a matter of fact, Dad said the majority did not want to fight, but they were forced to. It was either fight for your country or be killed. There really was no choice.

What follows is a captivating true tale of one family's survival during a time of war and depression.

Chapter One

Poland to Germany

Gottlieb's father (Alfred's grandfather) passed away when Gottlieb was only six years old. Then his mother, Regine, followed just six months later, from grief. So Gottlieb could remember very little about them; he was raised by an uncle. He also had one sister, who married, and, after having a couple of children, died at a young age.

What he did remember was that his father, Stefan, was very ill, quite often lying sick in bed. Frequently he would tell Gottlieb, "Son, come here and chase the flies for me." And so Gottlieb would stop playing in order to shoo the flies, only for his father to repeat the same plea again a few moments later. His father would often say, "If I get well, I will buy golden shoes for you to wear."

Gottlieb's parents lived in the district of Radom, located in central Poland, where the parents of Rosalie (Gottlieb's wife) resided as well. Rosalie's parents were Christian Kufeld and Karoline Knodel.

In the days of the nineteenth century and into the early twentieth century, parents picked who their children would marry. Basically, the young couple just shook hands upon meeting and married shortly thereafter. At that time it was common practice for land to be given to one's children as part of an offering for their marriage. Gottlieb inherited the farm owned by his father in Poland and was considered wealthy. Rosalie also came from a well-to-do family; it was rumoured to be one of the richest in town. Quite often the wealthy married the wealthy, as still happens in many countries today.

For the rest of her life Rosalie could remember the day she met her future husband. Gottlieb's uncle brought him by Rosalie's house while she and some friends were playing outside. She was 16. It would be a good match for the young couple. Gottlieb was small for a man (about 167.5 centimetres, or 5 feet 6 inches), humorous, honest and a straightforward person. Rosalie, on the other hand, was much more serious and very strict, slightly smaller than her husband and wearing her long hair up in a bun. She would always make sure her children were looked after.

Drafted into the army for the First World War when he was about 27, Gottlieb fought for the Germans. At that time he and his friend, Werner, were fighting in France (in Argonin) against the Americans. It was here that he had his first encounter with a person of a different race, a 'black man' as they called him. Upon seeing this man, Gottlieb and Werner turned and ran as fast as their legs could carry them, for they had never seen nor heard of such coloured skin.

Fed up of warfare on the front lines, the pair decided to wound themselves so they could end their fighting and go back to the *Lazarett* (army hospital). They conjured up the idea of shooting themselves. First they would fire through a red beet so the gun wound would not appear to be at such close range. Through the beet the bullet would go, entering into the hand of his friend and then the bullet would penetrate to Gottlieb's foot. Gottlieb would be the one to pull the trigger. His friend urged him on, yelling "Shoot, shoot!" but Gottlieb suddenly was uncertain he could pull the trigger. Werner became angry at his companion for losing his nerve. In exasperation Werner grabbed a knife and cut up his own hand. Gottlieb wrapped it in cloth for him. "Goodbye Gottlieb, I go," said Werner. Leaving Gottlieb behind in the enemy lines, he fled the scene. Gottlieb thought to himself, 'I don't want to shoot at the Americans, they did nothing to me.' He decided to follow his friend. Attempting to catch up to him, he sprained his ankle along the way; by the time he arrived back at army camp, he was unable to fight because of his swollen, injured ankle. It turned out that the First World War came to an end not long afterwards.

Both born in Poland and living in communities where eighty percent were of German descent, Gottlieb and Rosalie decided to move their young family to Germany. Gottlieb always believed that he did not belong in Poland. "When I heard the Polish language," he would later often tell his children, "I don't believe that I belonged there and I wanted to move to Germany where I could speak my own language with others." After investigating land in Germany that was being sold due to bankruptcy, Gottlieb travelled there to secure the property for his family. The bankrupt land was divided into several parcels, and it was one of these parcels that the Kienitz family would own.

Christian and Karoline were very unhappy that Gottlieb was taking their daughter and grandchildren away. In fact, they were downright mad. Gottlieb's barn in Poland had burned down and, although he had just built a new barn on his farm, Christian could not talk his son-in-law into staying. It would be years later that the Kienitz household in Pessin would be appreciated by Christian and Karoline and become their new home as well.

Having sold most of their personal possessions, the Kienitzes travelled by train in the fall of 1929 with few belongings and five children. Rosalie was pregnant with Alfred, who always jokes that he was made in Poland but born in Germany. When the family arrived at the train station nearest their destination, they travelled to the neighbouring village of Pessin, where they were greeted by a man who drove them to the farm. This person later told others, "Boy, *today* I picked up a family! All they had was a wagon full of children!"

And those children were: Erna (b. July 21, 1913); Else (b. November 18, 1916); Siegfried (b. September 9, 1920); Erich (b. May 18, 1925); Gustav (b. February 27, 1928).

With the money that remained after the down payment on their new farm, Gottlieb purchased two horses, a few cows and some chickens. The cows and chickens provided most of what they needed in the way of milk, butter, cream and eggs. It was a good start for the family in a new country where they were proud to be, a place where their mother tongue was spoken.

Although most homes in Pessin were equipped with electricity and running water, the first few years were very hard for Gottlieb and Rosalie. They had spent most of their money on the property and on items necessary for establishing a household. With many mouths to feed and much work to be done, there was little time for play.

Chapter Two

Alfred's Life Begins

On January 2, 1930, Alfred Kienitz came into the world. He would be the youngest son; a sister would follow and complete the family.

Since they owned so few belongings, many thought the Kienitzes would not last. They had no machinery to do their farming; in the beginning neighbours were reluctant to lend them anything in the way of equipment. To help the young family get started the government gave them seed potatoes, which was a tremendous assistance. Growing sugar beets, rye, oats, barley, wheat and potatoes, they worked relentlessly to obtain strong, healthy crops. Other farmers scoffed at the way the Kienitz family planted their potatoes. Gottlieb would steer one horse with a single plow to make rows for his potatoes and, instead of planting the potatoes further apart, would plant them close together to obtain a better yield. A foreman for the farmers' co-op drove by and, seeing Gottlieb's closely-planted potatoes, thought this was a strange way of planting. The foreman figured they would be overcrowded, and thought Gottlieb lacked experience in the farming department. He was to be proven quite wrong.

The family's perseverance and hard work paid off. Weather conditions were good that year. Rain and favoured warm weather, as well as their strong belief in God, produced plentiful farm crops.

As Christians, the Kienitz family would visit the Lutheran church in Pessin every Sunday. On no account did they work on Sundays; instead, after church the children played *Versteck und Suchen* (hide-and-seek) with their friends, or *Reuber und Schandarm* (robbers and searcher).

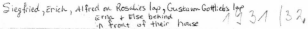

Siegfried, Erich, Alfred on Rosalies lap, Gustav von Gottlieb's lap
Erna + Else behind
in front of their house   1931/32,

l – r: Siegfried, Erich, Rosalie holding Alfred, Erna,
Gustav on Gottlieb's lap, Else – c. 1931/32

In 1934, on May 15, the last of the Kienitz clan was born. Alfred was corralled into his parents' bedroom. "Come and see your new baby sister." She was placed at the foot of the bed, a tiny bundle named Luise, affectionately nicknamed Liesel. This is Alfred's earliest memory, at the age of four. That birth completed the family of nine: the two parents plus Erna, Else, (Erwin died at birth), Siegfried, Erich, Gustav, Alfred, and Luise.

Front Row - Alfred lied on Rosalie's lap, Gustav.
Erich in front of Else Erna, Gottlieb, Erna

l – r: Erich, Alfred, Rosalie with Luise (pronounced Looeeza),
Gustav; in back are Erna, Gottlieb, Else – 1935

As the children grew, times were tough and everyone had to pull their weight to help out. In 1938, Gottlieb purchased a tractor, a Normack. It was the first tractor in the whole village. Gottlieb decided he would be able to get the work done much more quickly with such a machine. Again the townspeople had a good laugh. "Why would he buy such a tractor now?" they chuckled. But they didn't laugh very long; instead they came to him, asking him if he could do custom work for them. He even did a lot of work for the farmers' co-op, cultivating sugar beets and burying potatoes. Two machines behind the tractor were operated by two men, with Gottlieb at the helm. They accomplished much more work in much less time.

In the summer of 1939, Alfred went to the doctor, as he was experiencing pain in the lower abdomen. It was discovered he had a hernia; surgery was scheduled for August. With much hard farm work to do, Alfred always wanted to help out, and so probably developed the hernia from the heavy physical activity. He was just nine years old!

A neighbour of Alfred's, who was a few years older than he, had just gone through surgery herself after experiencing an accident. She began to fill him in on what he could expect during his time in the hospital, including the anaesthetic. She described a mask that would be placed over his face; this, she said, would make him go to sleep.

Once on the stretcher in the hospital, the worried Alfred looked above him, as he could see activity in the reflection in the lamp. His eyes were searching for the nurse who would place the mask over his face for the surgery. However, this did not take place. Instead the nurse gave him an injection in his right arm while his left arm was tied down. As the needle entered his arm, Alfred began to shout, "Ow, Ow!"

They told him to calm down and start counting. Initiating the count for him, the nurse finally had Alfred join in and he began to count as well … three … four … five …

He continued to count higher – to twenty, twenty-one … and then he was out.

Awakening, he found himself lying in a hospital bed feeling relieved that the surgery was over. He was not allowed to eat or drink for three days. To moisten his lips, the nurse would place a moistened face cloth over his mouth. Once the nurse left, Alfred would wring the face cloth and squeeze as much water as he could into his mouth. He complained of his hunger and thirst to no avail.

After three days he was finally allowed to drink tea; the nurse advised him to drink it very slowly. Alfred was so thirsty it was gone in no time. Every day, to heal the wound faster, a device resembling a large heat lamp would be placed over the incision for a period of fifteen minutes.

Alfred was healing nicely and was allowed to go home after 10 days. However, his family was too busy during the harvest to pick him up and he was forced to remain at the hospital. He was healthy enough at this time to begin walking around the hallways and the grounds of the hospital.

Alfred feeling better on hospital grounds – 1939.

Near the end of his stay, one of the nurses who had taken Alfred under her wing whispered to him, "Would you like to see an old man?"

With wide eyes Alfred replied, "Yes!"

She walked along with him to the end of the long hall where an old man was in a room alone, lying in bed. Alfred learned that the old man was 76 years old, very sick, and was going to die soon. In those days 76 was considered *very* old.

Alfred was apprehensive about seeing the old man. Walking very quietly to his room so as not to disturb the gentleman, the nurse and Alfred peeked around the corner from the doorway. Alfred froze as he saw the still man with white hair covered with a blanket up to his chin. The nurse and Alfred stayed only momentarily before turning away.

"Did you see him?" she questioned.

"Ja, ja," Alfred replied, still mesmerized by the sight.

The experience left him extremely saddened. There were no thoughts of himself growing old; rather, he felt great sorrow for this man who was at the end of his life.

Eventually, the surgeon had an errand that would take him past Pessin, and he told Alfred he could drive him home. Alfred had ended up staying at the hospital for 21 days! The surgeon stopped his car along the road for Alfred to get out and walk the remaining three hundred metres towards his home.

When he sauntered into the house, his family was shocked to see him.

"How did you get here?" they enquired.

"The doctor gave me a lift," Alfred answered, grinning.

They were ecstatic to have him home again, and extremely glad they didn't themselves have to manage the long trip to the city.

Chapter Three

The War Begins

Alfred was nine years of age when World War Two began. It was September 1, 1939. In just fifteen days, Germany had defeated Poland.

Siegfried Kienitz – 1941

Else, Gustav, Alfred, Erich, Erna – 1941

In the beginning, combat was off in the distance, in the countries of Holland, Belgium and France. Toward 1941 as the war raged on, it approached closer into Eastern Germany, where air raids happened nightly. Around 1943 there were air raids daily in the city of Berlin, as well as in other built-up cities where industries could be targeted and destroyed. Being only 55 kilometres from Berlin, the Kienitzes heard the raids very clearly. American planes flew in groups of twelve at a time and bombed the city mostly at night. Many planes took to the sky in combat. The civilians positioned blankets over their windows so no light would show out. Cars would mostly conceal their headlights when they drove at night; only a small narrow light was allowed to shine in the centre. For anyone who did not comply with these demands a fine was imposed.

The German soldiers at one time during that winter just barely maintained their front without pushing forward because of cold weather in the Soviet Union. German soldiers were unprepared for the cold, harsh winters and decided not to push farther into that country. They had problems with frostbitten toes and fingers with the improper coverings of boots and gloves.

The government pleaded with civilians for donations of warm socks, sweaters and gloves.

On a Sunday evening in the fall of 1941, Alfred worked on his homework in the kitchen, alone. As one would expect of an eleven-year-old, covering the window with a blanket as dusk fell upon the town was not the first thing on his mind. All of a sudden a loud banging at the door disrupted his concentration. It was a policeman, who began shouting about the light being seen from outside. The rest of the family was upstairs. Hearing the policeman's loud voice, most of them came running. Luckily, Alfred's brother-in-law, Otto, was visiting, and was able to calm the policeman down. Fortunately the family was let off with just a warning.

When the four alarms would sound, it was a signal that enemies were approaching. Civilians would take cover in bunkers. After the four long alarm warnings came, the next sound would be the continuous full alarm, similar to an ambulance siren. When the air attack ended, one long constant alarm would sound for about one minute.

In December of 1940 Alfred's oldest brother, Siegfried, had been drafted, at the age of twenty.

This was a brother with whom the young Alfred, in his few short years before the war, had shared much. Many times they had driven to the field together to get feed for the cattle. On one occasion Alfred was at the helm of the wagon, holding onto the reins of their workhorses. Alfred loved all livestock, but especially horses. And Siegfried loved to joke. As Alfred stood with reins in hand Siegfried, standing behind his brother, took a flexible measuring tape from his pocket. After extending it out, he began shaking it wildly, making a loud crinkling noise to scare the horses and make them run. And run they did! The spooked horses galloped at full speed. The wagon was flying on the dirt road, swaying from side to side. Alfred screamed with fright, trying to gain control of his horses, while Siegfried laughed hysterically.

One year and one day after his draft into the army, Siegfried's life ended tragically. Word came to the family by way of an army letter. The letter stated that Siegfried was shot and killed on December 3, 1941. His job was messenger on a motorbike, delivering and receiving messages from the front line. He was shot near the city of Tula, not far from Moscow. He was just twenty one years old.

WW2 Fallen Soldiers from the village of Pessin, population 800. Alfred knew 80 percent of the 56 names on this list.

Chapter Four

The Butchers

During the alarms, there were many nights Alfred and his father would stand outside their farmhouse and listen to the sound of sirens unfolding. Then the bombing would begin. The Americans would drop light bombs that would illuminate the air and ground, making it easier to find their targets. Alfred believed these bombs were attached to parachutes, as they descended from the sky at a slow pace. Once the Americans' target was established, a variety of different types of bombs would be released. Some ignited by impact, others would penetrate the roof right through to the floorboards. Some were lit up like Christmas trees as they fell burning to the earth. Father and son, standing side by side in great sadness and fright, could feel the vibrations of destruction beneath their feet.

In 1942, when Alfred was 12 years old, he didn't yet have the strength to do many of the farm chores, so his job would be to drive the wagon with the horses out to the field. Perched upon a straw-filled sack, Alfred would bring the wagon filled with manure out to the field for one of their two male Polish workers to unload, with tools similar to a hoe, onto the bare fields. He would then drive the wagon back to the barn, where their other Polish employee would reload the wagon with manure. This manure would be dumped on the field in small piles about eight metres apart, which made it easy to spread with a pitchfork.

These two young Polish men, Stanislaw and Bugei, who were in their early thirties, ate with the Kienitz family and shared a bedroom together. Gottlieb and Rosalie treated them like their own sons, and could converse in

Polish with them. Stanislaw arrived about three or four years before Bugei and they both stayed at the farm until the war was almost over.

Stanislaw, whom they affectionately called Stachu, was very talented with tools. He could make a ring using a silver piece of currency. He would take the piece of money, drill a hole in the centre and, using a special tool and a light hammer, bang it all around the edge, continuously turning the silver piece. The outcome would be a shiny polished silver ring. The Kienitz boys learned this art technique from Stachu and made a few of their own.

Bugei seemed to come from an uncultured community, and had not previously eaten many of the foods the Kienitz women put on the table. His very first experience eating white asparagus (there was only white asparagus available in Germany and it had to be peeled prior to cooking) was not pleasant; he immediately spat out the stringy vegetable.

Joseffa, in her mid-twenties and also Polish, joined the family about two years after Stachu. Her duties were divided between house chores and farm work. Eventually Stachu and Joseffa began a love affair.

Christmas would see very few gifts for all the Kienitz children. It was a poor time for all, but there were always gifts for everyone, even Stachu, Bugei and Joseffa.

All citizens were required by law at that time to fly the Nazi flag on certain occasions. The Kienitzes were one of only two families in their community that had not joined the Nazi Party. Rosalie despised flying the flag and all that it stood for.

This flag had been adopted in March, 1933, as co-national flag and in September, 1935, as the national flag of East Germany. White is the background of the black swastika; red encompasses the circle.

Once a week, Alfred along with six to ten other boys around the same age (12-14), would participate in a Hitler Youth Group. During the war there was a shortage of teachers, with just one teacher riding his bicycle every day to teach eight classes. In the large one-room schoolhouse lessons lasted three hours. When school ended at about noon, the children would go home and eat their *Mittag* (supper); at six or seven o'clock the family ate their *Abendbrot* (evening bread) open-face sandwiches. After Mittag the youngsters changed into their special brown shirts, each adorned with a black scarf that was held in place by a leather knot. On their left arms they wore swastikas. As Gottlieb was against Hitler, Alfred would place his armband in his pocket before re-entering the house after the Youth Group meetings were over.

The young boys would meet at the schoolyard at 2:00 p.m. for a couple of hours of light training. They played games such as hide-and-seek and tag. Usually one leader would conduct the young troop in a large classroom and give them a little taste of what army life would be like. Quite a few times they walked a few kilometres to a neighbouring village to conduct the meetings there.

In February of 1943 Alfred's brother Erich was drafted into the Army. Gustav would be drafted in the autumn of the following year.

Often when there was an animal butchered on the farm, the children would plug their ears and close their eyes for the horrible task. On one particular day in the early winter of 1943, the local butcher made one of his twice-a-year visits. Going into the barn, he tied a rope around the right back leg of a pig and walked the animal out. The barn door was then closed and the rope end was tied up very short onto the door hinge. Many people were involved as this was an enormous event that needed numerous hands. The pig was pulled, to force it to sit down, and then hit on the head with the flat end of an axe. At that moment Alfred ran out of the barn, covering his ears against the pig's anguished squeals. In this procedure the pig would fall to the right and the women would wait with an enamelled bowl to catch the blood. Meanwhile the butcher would kneel on the pig, lift up the left front leg, and pierce the animal with a knife, cutting the main artery. The blood would flow into the bowl held by one of the women. When the bowl was full, the butcher, using his hand, would plug the hole and wait for the bowl to be dumped. The process continued until all the blood stopped flowing. The fresh blood would be dumped into a pail where another woman continuously stirred it, to prevent it from thickening. The Kienitz family would make their own various types of sausage using this liquid.

Alfred did manage to return to the barn minutes after running from it and, despite such a traumatic beginning, eventually took up a career as a butcher.

Alfred grew quickly; at the age of fourteen he weighed 72 kilograms (158 pounds) and stood 167 1/2 centimetres (five feet six inches), the height he would remain for his adulthood. Prior to this he experienced pain behind his knees, so his mother took him to the doctor. The pain turned out to be growing pains, resulting from a growth spurt. The advice given was just to take it easy and not to overdo his physical activity.

In 1944 Alfred completed Grade 8. Middle school was not an option, because it was far away and transportation was slow. Middle school was only for those who had the funds and wanted a higher education to pursue a profession, perhaps to become a doctor, lawyer or teacher. Others would learn a trade after the eighth grade, which is what Alfred aspired to do. During that final school year a career counsellor would talk to the children about their future endeavours. They would be given several options, with a discussion on what was involved. Alfred determined he'd like to become a butcher, for he had often helped with that sort of work and enjoyed both making and eating the sausage.

With Alfred's career chosen he was eager to begin his studies. Standing in his way was Ferchland, the leader of the farm corporation for Pessin. Herman Ferchland, a farmer himself, belonged to Hitler's party and wielded considerable influence. He held periodic meetings for the farmers where they would trade ideas and voice opinions on farming concepts.

The oldest or the youngest son was expected to stay on the farmstead to help the family and eventually take over the farm. This was a Hitler law. However, war was war and every youth – whether an only son or one of four (as in the case of the Kienitz family) – was expected to join the army. With Siegfried killed in battle, Erich recruited and Gustav about to be drafted, it was Alfred's obligation to stay on the farm. Although Gottlieb would love for his son to stay and help on the farm, he wanted Alfred to have a trade, in case he ever needed to fall back on something. But Ferchland opposed Alfred's trade and wanted him to stay and fulfill his duties according to the law. If the son were to leave the farm for the apprenticeship, Gottlieb would need another strong person to help with chores. Ferchland was unhappy with the thought of having to supply Gottlieb with more farm help in place of Alfred. Gottlieb, being aggressive on this subject, disputed his claim and won the battle. In the end the farm corporation sent Tadeck, another Polish man, who spoke fluent

German, to assist on the Kienitz farmstead. Tadeck had a wonderful singing voice and would croon a tune upon request, even in German.

On the first day of April, 1944, Alfred started his apprenticeship in the city of Rathenow (pronounced Rutaknow). Oldest sister Erna, now thirty years of age, accompanied Alfred to this centre to explore potential butcher shops for her brother. The first store they chose was not allowed by the farm corporation, so the people at that store sent the pair to another place.

Erna and Alfred went for the interview to the chosen butcher, Otto, where it was planned that Alfred would remain for his three-year apprenticeship. Unforeseen circumstances shortened his time there to 13 months.

Otto Zupke was a large man of about 114 kilograms (250 pounds) – a good man, although strict. His wife was twice as strict. Otto explained that Alfred could eat anything he wanted, but stealing was not allowed. Otto was very good to the fourteen-year-old, and reminded Alfred of his dad in some ways – one of which was that they both liked neither Hitler nor the Nazi party. Two other youths worked alongside Alfred – a Czechoslovakian named Josef, and Erich, a German in his third year of apprenticeship. Erich was drafted into the army several months after Alfred arrived. Otto's younger son was in the army when Alfred began his training; he would survive the war. The oldest son was not as fortunate and had passed away before Alfred's arrival.

Six days a week Alfred worked tremendously hard while his boss maintained a rigid schedule. Many times Otto would wake him at 1:30 in the morning to begin making sausage. He would allow his young apprentice to nap at noon for a short period. In the evening many duties were left to Alfred to clean and tidy the store. When Alfred wanted to go home to his family on Sundays, Otto would ask, "Have you washed the floor in the basement? Have you cleaned this or that?" In the beginning, the chores were not always accomplished, but as time went on, Alfred became familiar with the routine. For some reason, Otto did not like to allow Alfred to go home for weekend visits. Home trips meant leaving the store early on Saturdays, about 5:00 p.m., and walking four kilometres to the train station for the 6:00 departure. This train would travel one and a half hours to Alfred's village where he would arrive at home by 8:00. When Alfred would ask again for permission, Otto would reply, "What do you want to go home for?" Being only fourteen, Alfred was homesick and felt terrible when Otto would practically make him beg to see his family. Many times he did not ask, as he was afraid to. Instead of requesting to leave early from the store, he departed on the Saturday evening 10:00 train. As that train did not travel to his village, it meant an eight-kilometre walk to his home. Walking home at the age of fourteen for more than an hour with nothing to light the way, Alfred was often scared. During wartime, houses were not allowed to have lights on. Windows had to be covered. The path was always dark and Alfred had to rely on his sense of direction to guide him home.

One spring evening in 1944, about five hundred metres from his home, a buck spooked him with a screeching noise. Although he knew what the startling noise was, Alfred ran like the wind to his house.

So, naturally, Alfred preferred to take the early train on Saturday evenings.

For the ride back to Rathenow on Sunday evenings, Alfred departed on the seven o'clock train, and would be accompanied by other teens. All the young folks usually sat in the same train car; long benches faced inward, so the teens were sitting opposite to one another. They would sing to pass the time. One boy played the accordion quite well as the boys and girls joined in rhyming songs about the various villages they passed through, many of the lyrics quite comical.

Chapter Five

The Shepherd

Late summer and early fall of 1944 was a tumultuous time for Alfred and his family, and for many others. A number of events took place.

Joseffa became pregnant with Stachu's child and in the winter of 1944/1945 she was sent to the city of Rathenow to give birth. Gottlieb fought hard to keep her in his house to give birth there, but the government ruled otherwise. Because she was forced – along with Stachu and Bugei and thousands of others – to work in Germany, she did not have many privileges.

Alfred owned a two-year-old German shepherd, not purebred, but a beautiful dog and very protective of his owner. No one could touch Alfred without Tieger (pronounced Teeger) standing guard. Alfred and his brother Gustav would poach for anything – rabbits, pheasants, all sorts of game. Not afraid in the least of gunshots, the shepherd accompanied the pair on their hunting excursions.

Every September, the German military held a draft for taking dogs in the army. Since the beginning of the war, no dog had been taken from the Kienitz farm – or any other farm around the area – for this purpose, as none could meet the high standards. The drafts were held outside, in a neighbouring village at a schoolyard. Required to go, Alfred approached the desk in the yard, where he proceeded to state all information needed – name of owner, name of dog, etc. – and walked away with a notice printed on paper. After all dogs were registered, owners and dogs went through a training test. Owners along with their canines remained in the middle of a large circle and one by one were assessed for their abilities. There were two soldiers who were well trained in handling dogs; one of them was equipped with a thick sack over his arm. He began to tease a dog, to provoke an attack. When the dog grabbed the sack, another soldier would shoot blank bullets into the air. One by one all of the dogs, when the shots were fired, would release their hold on the sack and take cover behind their owners. Even before it was Alfred's turn, his dog was extremely excited and ready to go. As Alfred talked to the dog and further built the excitement, Tieger would pull on his chain ready for his chance to attack. Tieger's agitation grew so much that Alfred had to calm him down a bit with a quick word. Tieger was exceptionally obedient and listened well to his master.

It took some time for all dogs to complete the test. Alfred's dog was about fourth out of 15 dogs to be examined. When Tieger's time came, he was again very excited and eager. The soldier lunged forward and smacked him with the sack on his arm. The shepherd jumped forward, grabbed the sack and would not let go. When the shots were fired Tieger paid no attention, and continued growling, holding fast to the sack even while the soldier shook his arm ferociously. It was only when Alfred gave the command to let go that Tieger released his hold. Another soldier wrote something on Alfred's paper and advised him to go back to the desk. After examining Alfred's paper, the desk clerk there informed him that the dog was to be brought the next day to the training station in Berlin. Alfred was in shock! If he had known what the soldiers had planned, he would not have enticed his beloved shepherd to be so fierce.

When he informed his parents upon his return home, they were also disappointed. Nothing could be done to save Tieger who, although fierce at the testing field, was lovable and protective of his family, especially Alfred.

In the middle of harvest, the Kienitz family could not send anyone with Alfred to Berlin. So at the age of 14 Alfred travelled with Tieger alone to Berlin by train. It would take up a good part of the day, a trip that was experienced with a heavy heart. The boy was told that if the dog did not meet up to their expectations, the army would return him. Even though Alfred had high hopes that his beloved pet would fail the army's requirements, the young boy cried for days afterwards.

In a letter sent after the four-week waiting period, the soldiers stated they were very pleased with the shepherd and the trainability the dog demonstrated. Along with the letter, the Kienitz family received a cheque in the amount of ninety-five Reichsmark. If the dog had been purebred with papers, the letter stated, they would have received much more money for it. The family never heard another thing of Tieger. Although the money was a windfall for the family, Alfred would have paid or traded anything for the return of his magnificent pet.

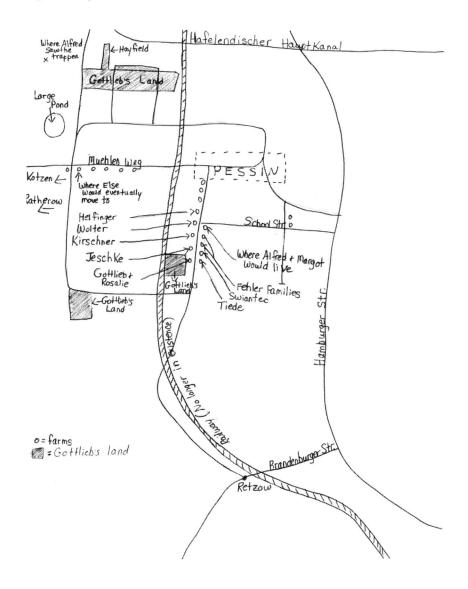

*Diagram of Pessin and area. Rathenow and Kotzen
are west of Pessin, Retzow is south.*

Chapter Six

The Bombs ... The Fighting

Not long after he lost Tieger in October of 1944, an attack came one day while Alfred was in Rathenow apprenticing. In the morning of a typical Tuesday, many varieties of sausage were being prepared. The last of the cooked sausage was taken out of the large kettle at 1:30 in the afternoon when the air raids sounded. Alfred, along with his boss and the co-worker named Josef, stood in the yard watching planes flying overhead. They flew in droves, in groups of twelve at a time, at high altitude. They flew in such a manner as a way to protect themselves. When the last group of twelve was flying over, shooting was heard from two light German planes attacking the Allies. The American planes quickly released bombs to lighten their load after this surprise attack. It was not a long fight. Alfred saw many American and other Allied planes plummeting to the earth. Several nosedived straight down, while others spun around with smoke billowing behind.

The city of Rathenow took the brunt of the released bombs and suffered greatly. Many buildings were hit, including Otto's house. Two light firebombs penetrated the roof and were wedged in the floor of the third level. The purpose of such bombs was to create a fire. About one metre long, five centi-metres in diameter, these bombs had six or eight corners, and on impact would start burning like a sparkler. Sparks flying onto wooden floors would quickly develop into a serious fire if not put out in time. Most homes were equipped, on the top level, with two large containers – one filled with water, the other with sand – along with a shovel, in case the home should be bombed.

At seeing the smoke from the two bombs that penetrated Otto's attic, Otto and Alfred quickly ran into the house and jumped the stairs two at a time till they reached the attic. Otto immediately grabbed each burning bomb and threw it out the window onto the road. The bombs were burning on the bottom only and were easily handled and disposed of. There were many fires burning. Alfred then went around the neighbourhood to assist with saving articles in homes for civilians in shock.

Before Otto's house was hit, one German fighter plane was shot down, watched by Alfred, Otto and Josef. Many of the downed planes Alfred observed that day happened to be in the direction of his hometown. He saw smoke billowing from behind the aircraft in the sky and silver gleams against the sunny background. His thoughts went to his family in Pessin and he worried for their safety.

On his arrival back home the following weekend, Alfred heard more news about the attack. His family said they and their neighbours had seen parachutes deployed. As these parachuting soldiers were specially trained, they disappeared without a trace. Many of the planes, Alfred was told, dropped in the neighbouring village near the Kienitz property. Alfred's parents explained that an American plane came down in one of their fields, so Gustav and Alfred decided to investigate. On their bikes they rode for about a kilometre to examine the wreckage.

Upon arrival, they saw pieces of metal scattered about. Items they found included a half-burned leather jacket, clothes and helmets. The most gruesome sight was a leather shoe with the foot still attached. The brothers felt very sorry for the people whose lives were lost in this battle. What came to Alfred's mind also were his own losses – his brother Siegfried and his brother-in-law Otto (Else's husband), as well as Erna's fiancé, who was missing in action and hadn't been heard from in some time.

Alfred heard more stories about the battle's aftermath, including one about a German plane that came down. When the plane was hit, the pilot ejected and landed on the other side of the village. The story goes that neighbours saw the soldier coming down but at that moment it was unclear if he was friend or foe. The mayor was notified and rode his bicycle with his gun to arrest the soldier.

When the mayor arrived, he discovered it was a German soldier. After the mayor questioned the soldier as to what his intentions were, the German pilot became quite angry at the mayor's intrusion. The pilot began lashing out at the mayor, telling him to leave him alone.

Around this same time, the German eastern front was pushed back because the Russian front was advancing. As a consequence of this, Alfred's relatives were evacuated from Poland. His *Opa* and *Oma* (grandparents), aunts, uncles and cousins were forced to leave their home. Among them was Siegfried Kufeld, a cousin of Alfred's who was the same age as he, and who wound up in Rathenow. Alfred's grandparents, Christian and Karoline, moved in with their daughter and son-in-law. Once very angry at Gottlieb for taking their daughter and grandchildren from the homeland of Poland, they were now extremely grateful for a safe and comfortable place to stay. A few months later, Karoline passed away. Alfred had hoped to get to know his grandmother better but, as he was living in Rathenow, he only saw her four or five times after she arrived at the Kienitz homestead. Christian remained with the Kienitz family until 1947, when he chose to live with his son, Daniel, who lived on a farm four kilometres away.

Chapter Seven

Erich At War

Erich's apprenticeship was from 1940 to 1943 with a blacksmith, working with machinery and shoeing horses. Like his brother Alfred, Erich lived at the home of a strict boss during this time. Shortly after completing his exam, in February of '43 he was drafted into the army for *Arbeitsdienst* (basic training). After four weeks of that training he was moved into the kitchen to assist the chef.

Many stories were shared when Erich's family came to visit him. Alfred and Gottlieb made the trip once during this training period, and Erich told them that near the kitchen facility there was a large airport where army parachutists trained for the war. These were Japanese soldiers fighting for the Germans. On one occasion after a jump, Erich witnessed one trainee whose chute did not open. The trainee screamed as he plummeted towards the earth. It was a horrifying sight, yet soldiers were not supposed to show any type of saddened emotion, so Erich swallowed his feelings. Upon relating this story to his father and brother, he only let his guard down a little, even though they were speaking in private. On the train ride home, which took almost all day, Gottlieb confided to his younger son that he could tell Erich was hiding much more of his emotions. Gottlieb knew his son all too well and saw the sadness behind Erich's eyes.

Erich enjoyed working in the kitchen and wanted to remain there. When it came time for selecting just a few assistant cooks to remain in the kitchen, his boss would have naturally highly recommended Erich. However, his boss had been away for a period of time and could not communicate this to the officials, so Erich was not selected. When his period of basic training ended, he was released and came home. Five days later, on the twenty-second day of May, 1943, a letter arrived stating he was to report to the army outpost at Kustrin, close to the Poland border. (Before 1945 Kustrin was a town in Germany on the river Oder. After 1945, a new border was established along the Oder-Neisse Line, and the city was divided between Germany and Poland.) From there he would be transferred to Frankford on the Oder for more training. Education for soldiers at this base was exercise for heavy artillery. Erich had many abilities and was put to work communicating with Morse code between the enemy lines.

As many soldiers were needed quickly, their basic training was a shorter period of time than usual. From Frankford, Erich's troop was transferred to Normandy, France, which is a half-island. Marching only at night so as not to be seen, the unit trekked for two weeks before arriving at the front lines, known as The West Front.

There was a declining number of soldiers already in action there. The new arrivals heard young boys of 16 or 17 wounded in action crying out in agony for their mothers. There were only a few left of the Hitler Youth Group after heavy firing took many young lives.

Erich was placed in a position slightly away from the line of fire but in a location where warfare could be analyzed. In a tent with a commander, Erich used Morse code, which was a viable means of providing highly reliable communication in the midst of difficult conditions. (Experienced operators could easily send 20 to 30 words per minute.) Using binoculars, Erich's team commander conveyed instructions to Erich and he in turn relayed messages in Morse, giving instructions to the other commanders as to where their firing should be directed.

During intense fighting a grenade landed near the tent and released a splinter that shattered the Morse code device Erich was working on. Erich was visibly shaken and considered himself extremely lucky to be alive.

In this heavy artillery area, the Germans were surrounded twice, breaking free each time. But the Allies' third siege was successful, and Erich and his unit were taken prisoner August 20, 1944.

Chapter Eight

Adolf Youth Group

In the fall of 1944, Alfred was one of a number of boys his age (thirteen or fourteen) who were sent a letter from the SS (the *Schutzstaffel*, or 'elite guard', the black-shirted personal guard of Adolf Hitler) requesting their presence at a meeting involving army information. He travelled by train from Rathenow to Brandenburg to attend the group meeting, held outside in a schoolyard. Three or four officers conducted the meeting, and once it was over the young teens were led individually inside the schoolroom where they had private one-on-one meetings with the head instructor.

When Alfred's turn came, he entered the school and found the young SS officer sitting at a desk with papers in front of him. The officer seemed very friendly at first, asking for Alfred's name and where he was from. He began questioning him in army form, very abruptly.

"What would you like to be in the army?"

"I would like to be a tank operator," replied Alfred.

"Why would you choose this?!" came the retort.

"Because I think I would like to drive a big machine like that and I very much like the black uniforms that they are wearing," Alfred responded.

The officer became very hostile and began yelling.

"Stand at attention!" he bellowed.

Alfred was shocked and numb from the officer's response. If only he could have left at that moment!

"Why do you want to be a tank driver?! Why don't you want to join the SS?!" the officer continued shouting.

Alfred's mind went into stun mode and he really didn't hear what else this angry officer was screaming. Alfred became very angry himself; he'd had enough of this official. He began to realize he should have told them what they wanted to hear, that he would like to be an SS officer. Alfred was finally allowed to leave the room to join the other boys in the schoolyard. He was hoping that he'd never have to face this man again!

In the first week of April, 1945 Alfred's boss, Otto, took a new apprentice under his wing. (All apprenticeships began the first of April, since school was out the end of March.) This adolescent was one year younger than Alfred. He was there only two weeks before he was called away to the Hitler Youth Group to be trained in shooting and to perform certain duties. But Alfred was not similarly called away. He was registered in Pessin but lived in Rathenow, so the authorities had lost track of his whereabouts. He felt very fortunate to have fallen through the cracks.

Chapter Nine

The Long Hike

In April of 1945, the Russian front line was coming closer to the town of Pessin. On the weekend of April 21-22, Alfred did not leave Rathenow to return home for a visit. With no newspapers or radio, he knew nothing of the approaching Russians.

Joseffa and her newborn baby were living in a work camp in Rathenow. In the late afternoon on Sunday, April 22, Gottlieb sent his employee Stachu, who was the father of the newborn, to Rathenow. Gottlieb instructed Stachu to go to the butcher shop and warn Alfred to come home and then fetch Joseffa with the child, so their family could reunite during this uncertain time.

Arriving by bicycle, Stachu immediately went to the butcher shop to notify the apprentice. Alfred was astonished to see his good friend, and greeted him with a wide smile. Not wanting to alert Alfred's boss, Stachu lowered his voice while he told Alfred the reason for his unexpected visit. "Your dad said you're supposed to come home, the Russians are very close," he declared in a quiet tone. Leaving Alfred the bicycle, he abruptly left to collect his child and Joseffa. As night approached, Stachu and Joseffa began to walk the approximately 30 kilometres back to Pessin with their young child in a baby carriage.

Alfred still needed to complete the day's work of unloading canned meat and sausage at the butcher shop, and he did this without alarming Otto. Once he had finished his chores, the fifteen-year-old sought out his cousin Siegfried, who was apprenticed to another butcher nearby, and relayed the news from Stachu. The pair decided to leave together that evening. Taking a few cans of meat and something to drink, Alfred left with his cousin around 10:00 p.m.

He did not inform his boss, as the latter would most likely not have allowed him to leave.

Siegfried had his own bicycle, and the two followed a rough bike trail alongside the familiar railroad tracks that Alfred had taken countless times on weekend trips home. Taking breaks a few times along the way, they opened up some of the cans of meat and rested momentarily.

The three-hour excursion was filled with apprehension. Travelling by dark and for the first time on this bicycle path, Alfred led his cousin to what he thought was a shortcut away from the tracks. It turned out not to be a shortcut at all, so the pair had to retrace their steps back to the trail beside the tracks. Pedalling through the dimness, they spoke little, in order to concentrate and conserve their energy.

Up ahead was a railroad bridge which was one kilometre from Pessin; *Volkssturm* (watchmen from the National Militia) patrolled this bridge that crossed over the manmade river called the Hafelendischer Hauptkanal. The lowland which stretched for many kilometres, even expanding to Rathenow, was an area built up to create better farmland and keep the area dry. The large river was about 15 metres wide. Designed to bring work to many during construction and keep those who were out of work off the streets, it was a prelude to the army for some, hand dug by men making seventy-five cents an hour. A small building which housed supplies for the river dam sat about 50 metres from the river. There the watchmen took shelter from the cold.

Alfred was quite familiar with this area. Many times as a young child he went swimming in the shallow river with his friends.

The cousins approached without hesitation. They were not aware of the watchmen on duty.

The walkway was now just wide enough to allow one to walk beside the railroad, on the opposite side of the tracks. Alfred and Siegfried, conversing quietly together, descended from their bikes and pushed them along toward the bridge.

A yell rang out from the opposite side. "Stop! Who is there?"

Alfred recognized the nasal voice and yelled back, "Are you Mr. Fenske?"

"*Ja*," came the reply.

Unable to see any figures up ahead on this dark night, Alfred quickly explained to Mr. Fenske that he knew him. The Kienitz family used to take their cows to Mr. Fenske's farm, where he had a breeding bull. The startled boys were told to advance further. When they arrived on the opposite side of the river, Alfred explained he was with his cousin and they were on their way home. Mr. Fenske said this was no problem and allowed the relieved cousins to carry on their way. They arrived home around 1:00 a.m.

The next morning Siegfried left on his bike for the seven-kilometre ride to his own house. Alfred was glad to be at home again, but more than anything his parents were glad he was safe. Stachu and Joseffa also made it home safely before the Russian invasion. Because they had a carriage to push on rough soil, they walked the whole way and arrived sometime after lunch the following day.

Chapter Ten

Soldiers and Weapons

Periodically over the next few days, German soldiers would stop and refresh with a meal or a drink at the Kienitz household. In mid-afternoon the day after Alfred arrived back home from Rathenow, a young soldier in his mid-thirties appeared. He had been in a group of soldiers to whom a command was given to recommence fighting at their post. The young soldier did not want to fight anymore, so he deserted and made his way to Pessin, ending up on the Kienitz farm. He wanted information on how to flee towards the west, and what was the best route to take.

Alfred advised the soldier to take the path along the railroad, the same path that he and his cousin had followed the night before. He explained that it was not well travelled, and deemed it to be safe.

The main road, about 500 metres away from the Kienitz home, at that time was called Berlin Hamburger Strasse. (Today it is known as Bundes Strasse 5.) Berlin Hamburger Strasse was lined with great oak trees, its branches barren now in the early spring season. Many civilians took flight from their homes on this road in the days leading up to the Russian Army's approach.

This particular day the road was quite busy. In the late afternoon, while Alfred and the German soldier talked freely behind the Kienitz barn, two light single-engine Russian planes approached to fire at the civilians travelling on Berlin Hamburger Strasse, who were trying to escape with their horses and wagons. The planes circled one after the other and dove down to shoot at the fleeing townsfolk.

At this shocking sight Alfred shrieked, frightened for himself and his family. Running to take cover near an apple tree, the soldier comforted the young teen.

"Don't worry," exclaimed the soldier. "They are not aiming at us; they are not shooting at us." He could tell by the angle of the planes that he and Alfred were not the intended targets. The intensity of the shots ringing out was incredibly loud and piercing to the ears and the spirit.

Alfred and the soldier ran into the barn and then to the house (barn and house were attached). A German soldier taking shelter at the neighbour's house across the road began shooting unsuccessfully at the planes. 'Dudududud dududud' was all one could hear from the planes for about ten minutes, until they finally flew off.

The soldier who had befriended Alfred left before dark. Rosalie, Alfred's mom, gave the soldier something to eat before he headed west. There was much commotion around the area of Berlin Hamburger Strasse where some civilians had been hit. Afraid for their own lives, the Kienitz family stayed put. The rest of the evening was quiet.

By late afternoon of the next day, heavy gunfire was heard regularly in the distance. Upon nightfall, the shooting became closer; the rumbling motor of a Russian tank was also heard far away. German soldiers, the Kienitz family presumed, were shooting at the tank. Moments later, the distinct tank motor was quiet.

Closer to midnight, Alfred was curious to see what was happening in town and told his father he wanted to check things out. His father, who was also inquisitive, gave permission to his son, telling him to be careful. Bravely venturing out on his bike, Alfred came to the main road that leads into town. The night was extremely dark; Alfred came quickly upon people in the middle of the road. Stopping to take in the sight, he recognized them to be German soldiers, one with a pistol in his hand. The three startled soldiers waited for their leader to speak, to ask Alfred what his business was there. Alfred explained that he lived nearby and wanted to know what was going on in town. The head officer told Alfred he had better get back home, as there would soon be gunfire.

Alfred turned tail and headed back home. Once there, he explained what had taken place, that all was quiet. No sleep was in store for many that night, due to uncertainty of what was coming. With everyone on edge, a good night's sleep was a distant dream.

It was around this time that the Kienitz family lost electricity to their dwellings. As a matter of fact the whole area was without power, and it was several months before power was restored. The whole town's water system was hooked up to the power source, so it was knocked out too. The family Tiede had a hand-operated water pump in their yard, which all the neighbours had to use to haul their water for many months. It was a tedious and difficult task, especially for those with several livestock and for those not living in the immediate vicinity of the Tiedes.

The next morning, which was a Wednesday, brought the sounds of more gunfire. Alfred and his family began to gather quickly into the basement once the gunfire grew closer. Mother, father, sisters Else, Erna and Liesel, along with Alfred and Grandfather Christian, were in the basement. There were other people present also, from a town nearby, friends of Alfred's parents.

It was a full basement, equipped with seven windows in various rooms, a fruit cellar, two potato rooms, a storage room where geese laid and hatched their eggs, and a utility room that housed the milk separator and large stone oven where bread was baked. Concrete floors and walls with ceilings, high enough for tall individuals to walk under, were built solidly under the large home.

Stachu, Joseffa, their baby and Bugei decided it was best for them to take shelter in the bunker located 60 metres away in the garden. Dug into the ground and constructed of wood supported with beams, the 3-by-4-metre bunker was covered with sand. The entrance was L-shaped and was situated so that if the bunker were to be hit by shrapnel, the rest of the bunker would be spared. Supplies kept in here were simple, with wooden benches and candles. Alfred's family rarely went into the bunker. Being out in the country when the air raids went off, they were not affected nearly as much as they would have been if they were living in the city, where most of the attacks were aimed.

At approximately 8:30 that morning, a soldier holding a machine gun sat in the ditch in front of the Kienitz property; a Russian tank that sat 500-600 metres away on the Berlin Hamburger Strasse was his target. "Dududud" was heard from his machine gun. The Russian tank shot back with a cannon that was deafening to the ears. For approximately 15 minutes gunfire was exchanged between the two sides. During that short time the Kienitz house was hit three times with blasts from the tank! Each time the house was rocked from a hit, screams could be heard from the terrified family.

One cannonball struck through the outside wall and hit a supporting wall, with shrapnel flying through to the first level of the house and into the ceramic cook oven. When this loud shot hit the house, the huddled family shrieked as the house shook. At this point Alfred's father became very upset at the German soldier, for putting his family in the line of danger. He had a good mind to go and tell the soldier to get out of that ditch, but he knew better.

Two hours had elapsed when shots finally grew quiet on both sides. Ten minutes passed, then another five minutes. Noise of the tank motor approaching was heard. The Kienitzes' dog began barking. Moments later, a voice called out in Russian, "Come out here." Dread filled the family with despair of what was to happen next. They expected the worst. Silence filled the basement. The Russian called out a few times more, with no one daring to answer.

"We have to go out," Alfred's father whispered. Alfred's grandfather, who spoke fluent Russian (as well as German, Hebrew and Polish), led the clan out.

Christian immediately began speaking Russian to the soldiers. "There are no soldiers here," he explained, and informed them of the German soldier who had been shooting from the ditch. The Russian soldiers appeared extremely nervous. The commander of the group ordered his men to investigate the property. During this time Bugei, Stachu and Joseffa emerged from their bunker and rushed towards the large group. The trio hollered in Russian and communicated to the soldiers as they approached that they had taken shelter in the bunker from all the gunfire.

Christian's knowledge of the Russian language seemed to put the soldiers at ease. The Polish trio's knowledge of Russian also helped to smooth things over.

The commander advised the family to take shelter back in the basement. "You don't have to worry about us. But be aware of the ones coming behind us," he warned. This comment indicated that conditions were about to get a whole lot worse.

Slowly, the tank resumed its journey down the road. Soldiers trotted along at a fast pace on either side of the large machine. Alfred and his family followed behind momentarily, to see where the soldiers were heading next.

A few hundred yards further along, they were met by another tank leaving the field and heading in the same direction as the first one. Moments later both tanks were out of sight.

Walking back up their laneway, the family saw tracks made by the first tank where it began its passage from a nearby bush. Crossing the field, where it plowed through a chain-link fence, it had approached straight toward the Kienitz house.

Inside their home, they found the devastation was minimal compared to what could have been. The family walked about in silence, measuring the damage and thinking about the events that had taken place since the gunfire ceased.

This was their first encounter with Russian soldiers and it brought out a variety of different emotions: excitement, anxiety, and fear of the unknown. What kept ringing through many a mind was the Russian's comment about "the ones coming behind us".

Further examination of the buildings revealed that the brick barn had been hit by cannon, most likely from German fire. The shot hit through a window in the hay barn and left a large hole. Other shrapnel left greater damage. One milking cow was hit by a splinter entering into her flank and exiting through the udder. She was badly injured but her butchering would have to wait, as danger was still looming.

The remainder of the morning brought more distant gunfire. Near noon fighting became even more intense, with shots resonating much closer.

The Kienitz family would soon find themselves in the crossfire of the Germans and Russians. The area between two fronts fighting one another is known as "no man's land". Shortly, unbeknownst to them, the Kienitz family would be in "no man's land". The afternoon would contain heavy shooting from both sides.

Chapter Eleven

The Russians Are Coming!

That same day, just a kilometre away at the manmade river Hafelendischer Hauptkanal, the Berlin Hamburger Strasse Bridge and the train bridge were the focus of shooting. Alfred and his family found out afterwards the Germans had blown up both bridges to prevent the Russians from crossing and entering deeper into their territory.

Rosalie and her daughters were frightened for Alfred's life. They had already lost their brother and son, Siegfried. Erich was in the war fighting on the Holland/France border and Gustav was in military training near West Berlin … When Else received her husband's belongings through the mail one day, she knew then that he had not survived; several weeks later she received a notice from the commander notifying her of Otto's death. Erna did not know at this point if her fiancé was dead or alive, as she had not received a letter for quite some time. It would be after the war that the family would search again for any word on Hans. Nothing could be established and so he was listed "missing in action".

Many strangers on this day were walking over the fields. It was not known what their motives were, whether they were thieves looking to plunder. So the Kienitz women felt Alfred should hide, to be protected. He appeared much older than his mere fifteen years so they feared he would be killed.

Alfred found a protected spot on the metal seat of a self binder (a machine pulled behind work horses to harvest grain) hidden by a straw pole barn held by strapping. He decided against hiding in the barn, which could easily catch on fire from bombs or shrapnel. From the metal seat he had a clear view of a bare field through which Russians might approach from the main road.

Some time had passed when Alfred spotted a Russian soldier on a horse, with a second horse beside him, approaching through the middle of this field. Quite by accident, a shot from a German cannon fired from the opposite side of the Hafelendischer Hauptkanal landed close beside the soldier. The horse carrying the rider halted, reared up on his hind legs, and threw the soldier off. Both horses darted away at full speed. Running behind the horses was the Russian soldier, anxiously looking around as if to dodge another shot. Alfred, quite nervous about this occurrence, watched until they were out of sight.

Not long after this incident, Alfred left his safe post – having first checked that the area was clear – and ran into the house. He wanted to share what he saw with his family, news at which his family became overwrought with emotion. Shooting remained heavy until late that night.

The rest of the night was fairly calm, as was the next day, Thursday. The odd citizen could be spotted running around, but mainly all was quiet. It was an opportunity to butcher the injured cow. As there was no refrigeration, they used what they could and salted the rest. The remainder was either sold to the townsfolk or given away by going door to door.

Salt is extremely important in a situation such as this, when no refrigeration is available. It enables meat to be preserved for much longer than would otherwise be possible.

Fighting remained very quiet until Friday late afternoon, when the opposing army arrived. The army and its equipment, horses and wagons littered the area, and the Kienitz property was no exception. The fields were full of excitement, with numerous soldiers scurrying about preparing for a head-on war.

Heavier equipment arrived Saturday. Cannons with shorter barrels, approximately six barrels connected together. They were known as "Katuscha". The Katuscha were extremely powerful, approximately thirteen centimetres in diameter; they were dug in behind and around the Kienitz property. Many varieties of fruit trees including plum, apple, sweet and sour cherries, and pear lined the property near the railroad. This was a wonderful spot for the army to station themselves, as they obtained a perfect view towards the river. There was distant shooting throughout this time, but it was mainly restrained. Alfred's family saw many soldiers scampering about with pistols.

Joseffa was approached by a Russian commander wanting information on how the Kienitz family treated her, Bugei, and Stachu. They wanted to know if they were being neglected or mistreated. Joseffa assured them she and the others felt like they were at home and could not have been treated any better by their own blood family. Joseffa later told Rosalie about her conversation with the commander, citing that if she had told him any different, the Russians would have killed the Kienitz family. Rosalie, shaken to hear this, was extremely grateful for Joseffa's revealing the truth about their close and caring relationship.

Through the commotion of the last several days, sleeping was naturally difficult. Before noon the following day, Alfred told his mother he was very tired. Rosalie suggested he go into the basement, where it would be quieter. Downstairs Alfred found a pile of clothes on the floor. He lay down, covering up with the clothes and fell asleep.

Alfred was not sure how long he had been sleeping when he was awakened by someone kicking him with boots and yelling, "Get up, get up!" Two officers grabbed him forcefully by his clothes, and were yelling in German, "*Warum bist du weggegangen, Soldat? Wo ist deine Pistole?*" ("Why did you run away from the army? Where is your pistol?")

Alfred's mother heard the disturbance and sent Stachu to the basement to assist Alfred. It was unclear whether the soldiers were Russian or Polish as they were wearing short leather coats. But the soldiers would not let Stachu speak; instead they yelled at him and chased him out. Stachu ran out faster than he had come in.

The officers asked Alfred for identification. Alfred reached for his wallet with shaky hands and opened it up to a number of photographs. In one photo, fourteen-year-old Alfred stood taking aim with a 22-calibre rifle. The soldiers shouted, "Oh, this is where you learned shooting? Where is this gun? Where is the gun?"

Alfred replied, "Oh, I sold it."

They continued searching the wallet and came upon a picture of Alfred's older brother, Erich, in army uniform. Upon seeing this photo, they asked, "Who is this?"

"This is my brother," came the reply.

"Where is he?" ordered the soldiers.

"He is in prison."

"Oh, good! Oh, good!" they shot back. Alfred was revolted at their happiness about his brother being in jail.

Tossing the wallet on the floor, the two soldiers disappeared into the next room, the fruit cellar, where canned goods were kept on a shelf. They helped themselves to strawberries and cherries, handing them to Alfred and loading up his arms, ordering him to carry the canned foods up the stairs for them.

At that moment, Alfred was so fed up he was ready to throw the canned foods on the floor. Everything happened so quickly, he did not have time to think. But even though Alfred was very angry, he knew he must carry out their commands or they might kill him.

The officers walked out behind Alfred, took the canned food from him, and abruptly left. His mother came to console him after this harrowing episode. From then on, no one would sleep during the day, for fear of more intrusions.

Christian owned a fine-looking pair of high pull-on leather boots. They were deep black in colour and came to just below the knee. It was around this time that a Russian soldier came by and saw these beautiful boots being worn by Alfred's *Opa*. The soldier wanted the boots and commanded Christian to remove them from his feet. Christian stubbornly resisted; the soldier knocked him down and drew a pistol. He proceeded to pull the boots off Christian's feet. He handed Christian his old worn-out army boots and put Christian's boots on his own feet. Christian simply took the soldier's old boots and threw them into the corner of the basement with great disgust. The soldier disappeared immediately.

About a day or two later, the Kienitz family was ordered to leave, as there would be heavy fighting. It struck Alfred that it was probably so soldiers could have more freedom to move into their home and eat their food. Since Christian was fluent in Russian and their Polish workers could also speak that language, the Russians likely ordered the evacuation because they did not want everyone listening in and knowing their business.

The family gathered up the most important items in a small two-wheeled wagon.

Stachu, Joseffa, their baby and Bugei also took a few belongings, some food and their baby carriage. They were planning to head to their home nation of Poland.

The Kienitz clan said goodbye to their trusted friends. They all hugged and wished each other the best. Alfred's sisters and parents told the trio to write or to let them know somehow where they were and how they were doing.

Because they had such a close relationship, Alfred and his family were sure that their Polish friends would make every effort to contact them after reaching Poland. They waited many months … but they never heard from their friends again. It seems certain the Polish friends did not make it to their home-land. The Kienitz family spoke often after the war about the trio and what became of them. They believed that perhaps Bugei and Stachu were forced to join the army. It was a very sad time.

Of the four horses that the Kienitzes owned, Grete (pronounced Greata) had been "drafted" by the German army the previous fall. The remaining three horses were now seized by the Russian army: the mare Puppe (pronounced Poopa and meaning "doll"), her three-year-old, Lotte, and a ten-week-old foal. Against their will, the horses were taken away. Half an hour later, the Kienitzes heard a noise at the gate. Looking out they saw Lotte had returned. It was assumed that the soldiers, attempting to saddle her, were bucked off and the young horse ran back to her home. Moments later she was seized again and taken away.

The Kienitzes took some food, their dog, clothing and important documents and headed south towards the home of Alfred's uncle (Daniel Kufeld), where Cousin Siegfried lived. Siegfried was the third oldest of eleven children. He had eight younger sisters.

The distance to Daniel's house was about six or seven kilometres.

The Kienitzes presumed it would be a dangerous journey, since there were many soldiers in the neighbourhood. They would be upon enemy territory with the Russians moving in, so it was agreed that only Polish would be spoken amongst them. This would better protect them if they were to be stopped and questioned. Since neither Alfred nor his younger sister, Liesel, could speak any Polish, it was best for them not to speak at all. The elder sisters dressed in old clothes and wore headscarves to make them appear much older. They also dressed their brother with a headscarf so he would not be recognized as a young man.

Moving along the main road, the family walked quickly towards 'Mud Road', a much less travelled path. They had to stop a few times along the route because Christian, Gottlieb and Rosalie needed to rest, not being as spry as the young adults. Luckily there were no confrontations, and they arrived in good time.

Alfred was fortunate enough to sleep in a bed with his *Opa*. The rest of his family, in his words, "slept like herrings, all in a row on the ground".

One night during the week-long stay, they were awoken around midnight by a woman running into the house, screaming. A Russian soldier was immediately behind, giving chase with a small flashlight. Christian became very angry and began yelling at the Russian. The soldier yelled right back, when all of a sudden Christian slapped him hard in the face.

At Christian's age, he was not afraid of the Russian soldier, and since he could fluently speak their language, he took it upon himself to take charge. Thinking quickly he shouted, "What do you want here? I'm an old man, and I want to sleep."

During this complete commotion, all family members stood up, realizing what was taking place. The poor woman, whom they could barely glimpse in the dark room, quietly exited by another door.

After a brief argument, Christian ordered the Russian to leave. Abruptly turning on his heels, the soldier left without another word. The Kienitzes never saw the woman again.

It was incredibly courageous of Christian to intervene for a stranger, to argue with the Russians about a woman he did not know. The younger members of the Kienitz clan were very proud and in awe of Christian's ability to stand up for justice.

Over the next few days the family spoke little of going back home. They wanted to be sure first that it would be safe enough to do so. The welfare of the livestock were on their minds, so after a week they packed up their belongings and once again headed out with their small wagon to make the five-hour trek back to their homestead.

Arriving at their farm around noontime, Christian walked into the house alone to speak to the commander, while the rest of the clan waited outside keeping a low profile. Christian explained that this was his home and property and he would like permission to re-enter. The house and property were swarming with soldiers. The commander agreed to allow them to stay – in the pig barn.

In the meantime, the family surveyed the whereabouts of their livestock; the cattle were roaming free in their pasture.

When Alfred found out from his father that they would be allowed to stay, but only in the pig barn, his reaction was, "What!?" Gottlieb's reply was, "You had better keep quiet; at least they are letting us stay."

Finding the pitchfork, Alfred began to clean out the pig barn to make accommodations for his family. By this time it was mid -afternoon. All of a sudden there was much commotion on their property. The Kienitzes began to wonder what was happening. Christian went to investigate, as the Russian soldiers appeared to be packing up their belongings. He spoke with some of them and found out they were moving on.

It was the biggest luck that the family could ask for! Perhaps the soldiers felt they would be intruded upon with the fluent Russian-speaking Kienitz family within earshot. The family waited around the barns, tending to various chores while the soldiers hastily gathered up their gear. By evening, not only was the house empty but the property was vacant as well of soldiers and once again full of the happy Kienitz family. Although their home had been invaded and was a terrible mess, they were extremely grateful to be back.

The following day they began searching for their cattle, herding them back home to the barns. Eight milking cows, along with their young and beef cattle, were 16-20 head. As the soldiers had used up most of the hay to feed their horses, Alfred began using a wheelbarrow to haul silage from sugar beets to feed the livestock. This silage was contained in an area covered with about 10 centimetres of *Kaff* (chaff). The *Kaff* is the leftover straw and hull after the grain has been separated out. The *Kaff* was then covered with 10 centimetres of dirt to preserve the silage. The reason for this is to seal the feed so it can ferment and be preserved. Later, when the feed was to be used, a spade easily slid under the *Kaff* to be lifted off to reveal the silage, which now had turned to solid mass. The livestock were in good condition, regardless of the fact the cows had not been milked regularly – or perhaps not at all.

With the power out and no running water, Alfred went to Tiede's farm to fetch water with his wagon. Once again, this would become a daily task.

Between the two homes of Kienitz and Tiede stood a stack of straw. On Alfred's way back with the water, he spotted a large sow munching on the straw and looking like she was nesting. The sow seemed to belong to no one. Hurrying home with the water, Alfred advised his father about what he had spotted. They both rushed back to capture the sow, but Tiede was at the scene and had in his mind the same objective. Alfred said he saw the sow first. Tiede knew that the Kienitzes often had pigs and agreed to let them have this one, as long as he could have one of the piglets when they were born.

Taking the sow home, Alfred and his father put her in a pen with straw. Later that afternoon she gave birth to three piglets. It was a shame there were only three, but at least the Kienitzes were able to keep two of them. The piglets grew fast and were very healthy.

Chapter Twelve

The Roundup

A few days later the Russian soldiers sent a German resident of Pessin, who spoke fluent Russian, to go from home to home alerting residents that the commander wanted every man, woman and child to meet at the village square in Pessin the next day at two o'clock.

When all the residents gathered in the square the following day, the commander spoke through an interpreter. He informed everyone that all women with children were excused to go back home, as were the elderly. The other residents were lined up in four rows, watched over by gun-toting Russian soldiers.

Alfred's mother and his younger sister stayed at home and did not even make the trek into the village. Christian, who had travelled to the village square with his family, journeyed home alone, while Alfred, Else, Erna and Gottlieb remained in Pessin.

All people were on their guard; not a soul knew what was to come next or where they were being led. There was much fear as Alfred and his sisters walked close together. The authoritarian soldiers did not feel it was their duty to give details of what was happening.

Some 40 or 50 terrified Pessin residents were marched for an hour on the Berlin Hamburger Strasse towards the next village, known as Saelbelang. There they were turned towards a field. In this open plowed field they came upon a few hundred workers using shovels to prepare an airstrip for Russian planes. Using as a carrying mechanism a piece of plywood about one metre by two metres, with a type of handle on each end, they loaded dirt and carried it 50 metres or so before dumping it to level out the uneven ground , to make it easier for planes to land.

Alfred had been given small mouth-sized pieces of a variety of bread by his mother before leaving for Pessin earlier in the day. Reaching into his pocket, he now munched on these hard bits of bread that had been left behind in their home by the Russian soldiers who had bivouacked there. Rock hard, this type of bread is eaten very slowly by sucking on the dense chunks. It was used quite often during the war because of its longevity. During that late afternoon it helped to ease Alfred's hunger.

"They (the pieces of bread) would last forever, they don't go bad! Alfred often exclaimed later. "Only thing, after a while, your mouth gets sore."

As nightfall descended, the group was not allowed to go home. The prisoners were marched to Saelbelang. When they reached their destination, before them stood a monster of a house of about three storeys, containing a large entrance and many wings and rooms. The Kienitzes knew this castle was owned by royalty before the war. (Just about every village sported a castle. In Alfred's hometown of Pessin there were two, one by the name of Wegener.) The Kienitzes assumed that the owners had either fled or perished. One of the owners of this castle, by the last name of von Wolfen, would come to the Kienitz farm to obtain milk a few weeks after the war ended. Gottlieb knew von Wolfen to be a good man. He subsequently disappeared; the Kienitzes heard later that he had escaped to West Berlin. Being wealthy, families like the von Wolfens left, as they figured they would be in grave danger once Russian soldiers appeared.

After a meal of warm but thin cabbage and potato soup, it was off to bed. When he was led upstairs to prepare for slumber, Alfred's eyes skimmed the room he was to sleep in with several others. It was a great shame that the once beautiful bedrooms looked more like stables; the bedrooms, now very primitive, were filled with mounds of straw. For breakfast the prisoners were again served the same diluted soup, lightly spiced and barely edible, before heading out to the field once again.

Soldiers searched for women to peel potatoes. Else and Erna, among several others, were recruited to this task. The sisters worked in the village barn, where they peeled and cut the potatoes before placing them, along with green cabbage, in a large cauldron. About a metre in diameter with a depth of about three quarters of a metre, the cauldron was made of enamel-coated steel. Normally used for boiling laundry, it now became a mega-pot of soup which would feed the field-clearing workers for a couple of days.

The next morning, back at the field, the commander approached the prisoners and spoke to them in broken German. He required men with woodworking experience. A number of men raised their hands, along with Alfred and Gottlieb and two neighbours of theirs. A group of 10 or 12 were loaded up on trucks and driven to the nearby woods. Lumber was needed to replace the bridges down on the manmade canal, the Hafelendischer Hauptkanal; these new bridges would be temporary bridges so the Russians could cross and continue fighting. Large trees were cut and the logs were brought back to the canal, about five kilometres away.

In the evening, the workers arrived back at the castle. Alfred asked Erna and Else how they had made out with cutting potatoes. No problems were encountered, they told him. Most of the soldiers were good men, but there were plenty of bad apples. There were guards in the evening keeping watch over the main door; rape was a large threat, especially when drinking was involved.

Alfred asked Erna and Else to inquire if the soldiers needed a butcher. At fifteen he was wise enough to come up with the idea of staying behind to work in the kitchen, close to his sisters. This would be much easier and safer for himself.

The following day, it was quickly arranged that Alfred would lend his talents at butchering and cutting up meat, and any type of prep work. That first day in the kitchen was very lax and light, and he just watched his sisters work. Alfred was great entertainment, making jokes with Erna and Else. They needed some comic relief after partaking in the craziness of the past few days (not to mention the last couple of years!); they also needed to take their minds off their mother and young sister at home. Thank goodness *Opa* was there with them! Surely he would let no harm come to them.

A day later an army truck arrived with four dead pigs. Helping to unload the pigs, Alfred befriended an older Russian soldier who seemed to know what he was doing, although his style of cutting was quite different from what Alfred was taught.

Left with the heaviest pig, Alfred carefully watched the soldier, so he could imitate him with his own pig. Placing the pigs belly-side down on the ground, the man placed straw on either side. The straw was lit and then held by hand to burn the hair off the pigs. Alfred began doing the same with his pig and, because he had never used this technique (Otto would place them in a tank filled with hot water to remove the hair), his pig began burning. The soldier became angry and yelled at Alfred. Realizing Alfred had not learned this method, he helped the young man with his heavy sow. Once the hair was burned off, the skin was left with a dark charcoal colour; they scraped the remaining hair with a knife.

Turning the pig belly-up on the ground, Alfred used a large knife to gut the pig. Looking up at his Russian comrade, he saw the older butcher cut the meat up from the outside without gutting the pig first. Alfred thought this was a little barbaric; it reminded him of a time he had seen a butcher working on a catch out in the wild, when as a helper he had accompanied a group of well-off men from the city on a hunt.

Alfred and the soldier finished cutting up the pig but, because the latter preferred to do it his own way, Alfred mostly just assisted.

A live steer at least 450 kilograms in size was brought the next day for them to butcher. When it was led into the barn, the experienced soldier shot the steer. Alfred was right behind, ready to take over its butchering. The soldier, seeing that Alfred was capable and skilled, left him to bleed, skin and gut the animal. Coming back periodically to check on the fifteen-year-old, the Russian soldier proclaimed, " *Kharascho kharascho!*" meaning *good job*. Once Alfred had the steer skinned, he had help with the cutting of the meat.

That evening, Alfred talked to one of his sisters to find out whether she would ask if it might be possible for him to go home, in that he wanted to see his mother. Upon her enquiring, the commander hesitated. He was afraid Alfred would not come back. Alfred had gained some trust with the soldiers and they liked the boy very much. Even though not everything was understood, due to the language barrier, they joked quite a bit. The commander eventually agreed, under the condition that his sister would guarantee Alfred's return the next following morning.

With a handshake promise, Alfred left late afternoon the next day, running most of the way. He was extremely anxious to see his mother.

He discovered back home all was well, with his *Opa* looking after everything marvellously. Alfred explained that he needed to go back the following morning, or the Russians might do harm to his sisters, but his feet were sore. Blisters covered his painful soles, partly from his shoes and partly from not bathing or changing socks. He soaked his feet that evening in a basin of warm water. In the morning he ate a hearty breakfast of smoked sausage and departed on the journey back to the "camp". He was a little leery of meeting up with additional soldiers along the way, soldiers not from the group he had been with the previous four days, but, luckily, that did not happen, and he arrived safely back at camp.

Alfred sought out the commander who had allowed him to go home. Shaking his hand, the Russian smiled from ear to ear, glad that Alfred had kept his word.

From then on, for the next couple days, Alfred's life in the kitchen was fairly easy. There was an older woman, who lived two villages away. She seemed to be the head cook in the kitchen and she took to Alfred right away. They talked endlessly, laughed lots, and she allowed him to pick away at the meat, permitting him to eat as much as he wanted!

As the temporary bridges were now built, the front began to advance once again. The soldiers, now on the move towards the river, did not need the prisoners anymore, and set them free. Alfred and his sisters were overjoyed at the thought of being reunited with their mother, sister and *Opa*. It had been three weeks since their roundup.

Built for emergencies, the airstrip that they worked on so tediously was never used!

Families went back to their loved ones. All was calm on the Kienitz homestead. It was time for Gottlieb and Alfred to 'find' some of their 'buried treasure'.

During the time Alfred was in Rathenow, his father, being incredibly wise about what might come in the course of the war, had buried many items to hide them from the soldiers – including clothes, dishes, and a 22-litre milk can filled with sugar. The Russians, aware of such tactics, uncovered many of the wooden boxes hidden by Gottlieb and others, as they walked along poking the ground with a long steel sword. The Kienitzes now had problems finding the remainder of their buried treasure! Alfred assisted his father by searching for the items with a long piece of thick wire. Just twenty centimetres in diameter, the milk can was difficult to pinpoint. Gottlieb was in the right vicinity, had not measured it out exactly. Alfred commented to his father that he should have calculated it more accurately. Gottlieb pointed out that he had to bury the cans and boxes quickly and alone, with Alfred being away in Rathenow. After much persistent searching, the pair finally found the can of sugar with extreme delight.

With the war still ongoing, the front began to advance. A few days later, Alfred and Gottlieb journeyed down to where the temporary bridges had been built on the river. As they began to come closer to the bridge, their eyes met a disturbing sight. Dead horses lying in the field, overturned train cars, craters in the land from the mortar shells ... It was a sad and disgusting display. They assumed that in the previous weeks, heavy fighting took place in the very place where they now stood. Train cars that lay on their side were probably pushed over intentionally for protection from enemy fire.

Chapter Thirteen

The Friendly Russian Soldiers

It was around the time just before the end of the war when five Russians, one sergeant with four other soldiers, moved into a home across the road and kitty-corner to the Kienitz farm. It was the home of Alfred's godfather, Adolf Sviontec, who occupied the place with his wife and three children, two of whom were then active in the war. Adolf and his wife spoke fluent Russian, so the soldiers became friends with the family and made this their 'homestead' during the end of the war.

Adolf's youngest child, Gerhard, fought in the war and eventually became a prisoner. The second child, a daughter, managed to escape during the war; it was believed that she worked as a nurse for the army in the west part of Germany. The son and daughter eventually came back home a couple years after the war ended. The eldest child remained at home with her parents throughout the war.

The duty assigned to the Russian soldiers was to manage cattle and dairy cows at the Sviontec home. During the time when families escaped, most animals were left behind. Horses were used as their means of transportation, but all other livestock were left. These Russian soldiers gathered up thirty-seven head of cattle that were abandoned by the escapees, and maintained them at Adolf's farm.

The majority of the cattle were milking cows and it was the duty of the Sviontec and Kienitz women to milk them. After separating the milk from the cream, butter would be produced and consumed by the five Russians and Sviontec family. The remainder of the dairy products was then shipped to the army base for the Russians.

Grazing in the pasture, the thirty-seven cattle, along with three horses, were kept watch of by Alfred and his neighbour, nicknamed 'Bohnert', who was a small-framed boy. He was one-and-a-half-head shorter than Alfred, although the same age. The husky Alfred dwarfed his friend! A whistle was given to the pair to alert the soldiers of any danger lurking.

Alfred and Bohnert used telephone cable to fashion a couple of home-made harnesses and were soon riding the horses on many a fun journey. On one such ride they were seen by one of the Russian soldiers, who showed obvious disapproval and told the pair to stop clowning around. However, it wouldn't be long before the boys were back at it again.

Quite quickly, the five Russians became very friendly with the Sviontec and Kienitz families. They became like brothers to Alfred, who acquired enough of the Russian language to share small conversations and jokes with them.

On one occasion when the boys were tending their own cattle they noticed another herd in the distance, slowly approaching. As the other cattle came closer the boys became uneasy with this situation, but never took their gaze off the potential threat. Noticing that a stranger was herding the cattle in their direction, Alfred became anxious and began blowing his whistle profusely until he saw one of their soldier friends riding out to them on his bike. The Sviontec farm was about 300 metres away from where Alfred and Bohnert were. By the time their Russian soldier friend arrived, the stranger had managed to mix his group of cattle with theirs in order to steal some of their livestock. He was already edging stealthily away with a few of Alfred and Bohnert's cattle in tow.

When the Russian soldier was close enough he asked the frightened pair of boys how many cows had been stolen, Alfred used his fingers to show seven had been taken. As the cattle were not moving too quickly, the Russian soldier caught up with and confronted the stranger. What followed was a shouting match between the two – who, it turned out, were *both* Russian soldiers. A huge argument ensued, but the Sviontec soldier had the upper hand. Alfred thought they were going to begin a fist fight, they were both so angry. Eventually the second soldier began to calm down and Alfred and Bohnert assisted their friend to reclaim their cattle. Whether they retrieved the right cows, no one knows, but they were able to walk away with thirty-seven head of cattle.

Speaking in broken Russian, Alfred explained laughingly that they had traded seven of their smaller cows for seven larger ones that belonged to the stranger. The Russian laughed along with Alfred and Bohnert, saying they had done well and he was very proud of how the young teenagers had reacted.

One early morning a few days later, Alfred went out to do morning chores. Still in a sleepy daze as he walked out from the back of his house towards the barns, he did not notice a Russian soldier lurking near the front of the house, next to a horse and wagon. Alfred was in the hay barn hauling feed for the cattle when he heard one of his sisters scream. His sleepiness soon left him as he ran to the entrance of the barn to see a man scurrying out from their basement door followed by his two shouting sisters. The soldier had apparently entered their home unnoticed and stolen two suitcases which contained the clothing of Erna and Else. The clothes were left in suitcases as a precaution, in readiness for a quick exit in case of emergency.

Fleeing as fast as he could, the Russian soldier threw the suitcases in the back of the wagon, where his cohort awaited with reins in hand. He hopped up and they made off in galloping tempo with their small horse taking the lead.

One of the sisters, acting on impulse and desperation, ran over to the Sviontec house to alert the friendly Russian soldiers that their suitcases had been stolen. One soldier ran out so fast, he was half-undressed. His suspenders were hanging down; he wore no jacket, just a shirt — but he carried his gun. This was the oldest of the soldiers, estimated to be in his late fifties. He was warmly known to his hosts and the Kienitz family as "Grampa" (or, in Russian, pronounced Dah-Doosh-Ka").

When he came running, the Kienitz group was standing in front of their home peering after the escaping thieves, who fled north towards the centre of Pessin. When they approached a "T" intersection in the road, 600 metres from the Kienitz home, they headed west, making a left turn. Here, the wagon was able to go at full speed on the smooth gravel road. Alfred figured then that they were headed towards the bush, where another Russian army kept post.

Excitedly, Alfred told Grampa where he thought the thieves were headed. They could see in the distance the road where the wagon travelled. Alfred and Grampa took off toward the north on a different road, one that ran along behind the Kienitz property. The pair ran fast, hearts beating wildly, the older man struggling to keep up with the fifteen-year-old. They caught sight of the wagon turning in a westerly direction and coming towards them. The wagon slowed down immensely on this next path, which was nothing more than a field. Rain the previous night had saturated the earth, leaving puddles and deep mud ruts that presented a difficult ride.

About 200 metres away from the wagon, with the determined Grampa and his young cohort still running northward, Alfred yelled out to his friend, "Shoot, shoot!"

Alfred wanted the gun so he himself could shoot at the thieves, but wisely the Russian soldier took matters into his own hands, and shot into the air. Three shots rang out. Panicking, the pair on the wagon whacked at their horse to run faster. The small horse took a few more steps then came to a complete halt. It was exhausted and just couldn't go any further.

Frightened, the pair then jumped off the wagon together and ran in a northwesterly direction, leaving everything behind, including the suitcases. The terrified thieves did not own a gun and ran for their lives towards the bush, where another Russian army had set up camp. It was believed that these two were part of the thousands of soldiers at that bush camp.

Alfred ran to the wagon, impatient that his legs could not carry him faster; Grampa tried his best to keep up with him. Not able to communicate a whole lot, the pair shook hands, laughed and made a few jokes about the incident. Grampa was very proud of his young friend for protecting his family's belongings.

Climbing up on the wagon, they made their way slowly back home with the fatigued horse in the lead. Along the way, Alfred felt especially satisfied with retrieving the luggage. It was practically the only clothes the sisters owned. With everyone's quick response to the thieves' actions, a lot of heartache was avoided.

Upon their arrival back home, the Kienitz family and soldier friends were waiting for them. Alfred's sisters were overjoyed to have their clothes and luggage returned. They repeatedly thanked their brother and Grampa for their valiant effort.

The Kienitzes and the friendly Russian soldiers were now in possession of a stolen horse and wagon. The horse and wagon in fact belonged to the neighbour of the Sviontec family. Word had it that the thieves took them the evening before. When Alfred returned the horse and wagon to the rightful owner, he was extremely grateful. It was a situation that helped to intensify the bond shared between the neighbours, the Kienitz family and the five friendly Russian soldiers.

A few days later, with Alfred and Bohnert tending to the cattle once again, Grampa approached the pair in the field, carrying his rifle. The pair, at first unaware of the reason he was carrying a gun, soon understood it was for a calf they needed to shoot for meat. Grampa chose a calf from amongst the herd, a calf which weighed about 250 kilograms. Facing the calf head-on at a range of about 30 metres, Grampa raised his rifle and fired — but he missed!

With a blank disappointed stare, he looked at Alfred with raised eyebrows and motioned to the fifteen-year-old, saying, "Come here. You shoot."

Surprisingly, the calf was still in the same spot and hadn't flinched one bit from the deafening gunshot. Alfred gladly accepted the rifle, raised it to his eye and took aim. He shot the calf squarely in the head.

"Good, good!" commended Grampa, who then took over the skinning and gutting, right in the field. Alfred and Bohnert carried on tending to the cattle.

With all the spring rain they had that season, the cattle that were normally kept overnight at the Sviontec yard (which offered the best protection against thieves), were moved to the higher yard of the Kienitz family, where the land was waterless. The Sviontecs' place had become too muddy for the cows to remain there during the night, so they were herded to a desiccated area for a while, just to dry up their usual enclosure. The pasture in the daytime was not a problem, as it was large enough for the cattle to roam under the watchful eye of Alfred and Bohnert. This daytime pasture consisted of six neighbours' fields of one hectare for each farm.

Grampa was the night watchman for the cattle. During the few nights that the cattle were in the Kienitz yard, he wanted Alfred to assist him with the task.

As the barn was attached to the Kienitzes' house, Grampa told Alfred he could lie down in the back bedroom closest to the barn, If needed, Grampa would signal Alfred to come. This bedroom belonged to Alfred's parents (the same bedroom Alfred was born in), so Gottlieb, Rosalie and their son lay down and went to sleep, Alfred with his clothes on. Grampa sat on the stairs leading into the house, just a few metres away from where Alfred slept.

Shortly after midnight, the Kienitz dog began to bark. Four strangers were approaching with the intention of stealing some of the Kienitz cattle. Not sleeping too soundly, Alfred was awakened as the barking began.

Grampa and the uninvited guests began shouting at each other, with Grampa pointing his gun at the intruders. Alfred, wanting to aid his friend, was promptly prevented by his mother, who thought it was too dangerous for him to go out of the bedroom. She was afraid he would be hurt – or worse – in this heated argument.

The yelling continued for some time, before voices were lowered and the four strangers ultimately left. The rest of the night descended into dawn without incident. It was destiny that the thirty-seven cattle, along with Gottlieb's livestock, were all at the Kienitz farm that night under the watchful eye of Grampa. If Grampa had not been there the consequences might have been serious. It could have ended up with missing livestock or, severely worse, a fatal ending had Gottlieb and his son been the ones to confront the four strangers.

1946/47 – The Kienitz barn, on left, was attached to the house in background. The first open door in foreground was the horse barn, second door was the cow barn; the pig barn was located closest to the house. Notice the air vents on the upper level of the barn. On top was the hayloft, stacked loose.

Chapter Fourteen

The War Ends

It was an unsettled time when the Kienitz family found out that the war had ended. With much looting in the area, it was certain that things were to become worse. There was a gang in town that looted night after night. Even one of the police officers was involved with the gang. He was more or less standing guard for his fellow looters. On one occasion they wanted to steal a pig from Else's in-laws (Otto and Minna Krueger). A neighbour walked home and saw the officer but did not think anything of it. After the neighbour was out of sight but walking towards where they wanted to steal the pig, the police officer let off a warning shot into the air. In the end, the thieves could not steal the heavy pig. The pig was discovered the next morning behind the barn ... and all the unsolved pieces fell into place.

Even though the war had ended, trouble was *far* from over.

The Sviontecs announced a few days later that the five Russian soldiers would be pulling out. They would be taking all 37 cattle and the three horses.

Alfred's parents and sisters became afraid for Alfred. Although the Kienitz and Sviontec families were friends with the five soldiers, they feared the soldiers might try to take Alfred and Bohnert to assist with the herding of the cattle back to their homeland. Alfred's sisters suspected that if this were the case, he might never be seen or heard from again. One could say Else and Erna's senses were heightened at the prospect of the Russians leaving with some accompaniment.

With the co-operation of the Sviontecs, it was decided that Alfred would sleep in the straw barn that belonged to the Sviontecs. Alfred would be safer if he was not on his own property. The Russians would not know to look for him in their own domain.

That evening Alfred prepared for what would prove to be a mostly sleepless night lying in an uncomfortable bed of prickly straw.. Cattle noisily called to one another while he slipped into slumber. After an hour or so, someone appeared in the barn, stayed momentarily and left. Heart beating fast, Alfred stayed alert for a period and listened for anything unusual.

Alfred left the barn early before daylight, so he wouldn't be seen, to go back across the road to his own home.

From their main base, an army truck with several soldiers arrived at the Sviontecs'. Alfred remained hidden in his own home, so he was unable to view much of the day's events.

The day seemed to go along smoothly, with the soldiers packing up their gear in the army truck and anticipating their journey. Readying the cattle, the soldiers began 'driving' the herd towards the east, back to the Soviet Union. The Sviontec family had their home to themselves once again.

The next several days went by without any commotion.

Alfred's eyes were always roaming when he was outside, looking for anything unusual, wanting to keep his family safe. One day he caught view of two young horses, about two years of age. Alfred approached the horses slowly, talking to one. He managed to catch her and brought her back to the barn. The other one followed. Alfred's father was very proud of his goldmine find, since the family's horses had all been taken by the Russian Army, leaving them with none for working the fields and no transportation.

Alfred decided one day to visit his uncle and the family they had stayed with a month earlier, which was a six- or seven-kilometre trek. He and his cousin Siegfried walked around to see what was happening in the area. Venturing out into the pasture, they came across many horses – twenty or thirty, most of them very young! The pair attempted to catch them and were successful with one, a quiet horse. He was about two-and-a-half years old, heavily built, a Belgian type of workhorse.

Bringing the horse back to his uncle's place, Alfred spoke to his uncle about his great catch. He wanted to keep the heavy workhorse, but his uncle traded with him for an older mare with a foal. Alfred accepted this decision, and, anxious to begin his journey home, said goodbye to his cousin, mounted the mare and was off. Following close behind was the young foal.

Alfred was relieved when he arrived home once again, having met no traffic other than a few scattered soldiers off in the distance. He was extremely happy with his new horses. His family was also quite happy and very proud. The horses would be very helpful around the farm, so long as no one tried to steal them again! Every door in their barns was always locked from the inside, so the only way potential robbers could enter would be to break one of the doors apart.

Chapter Fifteen

Leo

Alfred's cousin, Lena Arendt, and her husband, Leo, were the family of Alfred's mother. Lena's mother, Wanda, and Rosalie were sisters. (At this time of writing, in 2011, Leo passed away at the early part of 2011, in his 100th year. Lena is in her early 90's.)

Leo and Lena, as well as some of their immediate family, were living in Poland before the war. Since Leo was involved in the fighting, they were separated during the war; through letters there was a pact that if something should happen, they would all meet at their *Tante* (Aunt) Rosalie and *Onkel* (Uncle) Gottlieb's home. Leo arrived first in the summer of 1945. Lena, her three children (two daughters and a son), her brother (who was excused from the army due to a handicapped foot), her parents (Alfred's grandparents came in the fall of 1944 after being freed due to their age) and Leo's parents were in refugee camps in Germany. Later that year, they were released and were reunited with Leo in Pessin. Only Alfred's brother Siegfried, his brother-in-law Otto Krueger, and his brother-in-law-to-be, Hans Gruetsmacher, would never make the trek back home.

Leo's father liked to smoke, and rolled his own cigarettes. As there was not much paper in those days, he used – sparingly – the pages from the Bible for rolling his cigarettes. He used to say that by using that paper, he not only read the Bible, but also inhaled it!!

In his early thirties Leo was in good shape; his presence was very much needed on the Kienitz farm at this time. He, Gottlieb and Alfred went out working in the fields. With many Russian soldiers looming about, it was necessary and a great protection to have more than one presence in the field. While

Alfred drove the wagon with two horses (somewhere they acquired another one in addition to the mare Alfred obtained from his uncle) to a distant field, his father and cousin would sit nearby, alert to any uncharacteristic behaviour. The field had a slope to it; when Alfred was at one end of the field, his family lost sight of him.

Near the end of the day, Alfred's eye caught something.

"Look! Down there!" Alfred pointed to the distant sight of three horses walking on the other side of a ditch. No person could be seen in the area. "I'm going to go down and get them."

During this time many animals were captured and stolen, so it was not unusual to see animals roaming in the wild once they broke free.

Leo assisted Alfred; the pair walked together with a rope towards the horses. As they approached the ditch, the horses stopped while Alfred and Leo began talking to them in a friendly tone. The ditch was at least two metres wide, but they noticed a hole with a spade close by. Someone had used the spade to throw soil into the ditch, so as to cross without falling in. They both crossed over here and walked closer to the horses. Just by glancing at them one could see these horses worked together, had always been together. Two were light brown, the third was lighter in colour and also in weight.

Approaching slowly and able to pat the horses now, Alfred gently positioned the rope on one horse, to use as a halter. The others would follow. Alfred crossed the ditch first with the horse seemingly in tow, but the horse was afraid to cross over and held back.

"Just hold on a minute," exclaimed Leo grabbing the spade. With the flat side of the shovel, Leo smacked the horse's rear. In a split second the horse was over the ditch, followed by the other two horses. Their bond was so strong no water or ditch could separate them. As proud new horse owners once again, Leo and Alfred led the new-found livestock back to the farm.

The Kienitz horses were not in good shape, due to lack of good food. Because the horses just captured were in better shape, they were put right to work. Changing the harnesses of their own horses with the two heavier horses they had just acquired, Leo, Alfred and Gottlieb brought these new horses to the field to carry on working the ground preparing for the seeding of beets.

In the evening, a discussion ensued regarding the fate of all the horses. They were not all needed and it would pose a problem to feed them all. Alfred suggested going to their second neighbour's house to see if they could use one. Those neighbours were more than happy, quite enthralled actually, as they had no horse. Alfred brought the light-coloured stallion, the one in the group of three he'd found, to their neighbours' place, and was quite pleased to be able to give it to them.

Two days later, still working the field with the new horses, Alfred and his father laboured together. Their own horses, still weak and undernourished, were resting in the barn. Alfred was over the slope, out of his father's sight, when a Russian soldier on horseback appeared around the corner. Because of the way the land sloped, neither Alfred nor the soldier saw each other, but the soldier saw Gottlieb. Stopping to talk to him, he asked Gottlieb if he had seen three horses in the area.

"No, no horses," came the quick reply.

In the meantime, Alfred appeared over the hill with the two workhorses. If Alfred had seen the soldier before the soldier saw Alfred, he would have turned on his heels in the opposite direction. As he approached, the Russian shouted out, "Those are mine, my horses!" Enquiring more, he asked if they had seen a third. "No," was the reply once again. It was bad enough the soldier was about to confiscate the two horses; they did not want to give up a third.

Because Gottlieb could speak well with the soldier, he asked him if Alfred could go home to retrieve their own horses and exchange them for his. Acting extremely nice, the soldier agreed to let Alfred go and Alfred was off right away for the barn, a good half-hour's walk.

In the meantime Gottlieb, having a good conversation with the Russian, asked him if he could get Gottlieb a horse. The soldier, wanting to strike a deal, agreed. Gottlieb explained where they lived and, sure enough, two days later the soldier appeared with a horse. (Alfred was actually disappointed with this deal, as the horse had a skin disease.) In return, Gottlieb gave the soldier a young foal, along with some other considerable offerings of alcohol or money. Nothing was ever said about the third horse again. The neighbours kept that horse for many years and it turned out to be a great stallion for them.

Chapter Sixteen

The Steer and Typhoid

In the latter part of May, 1945, Gottlieb made a deal with some Russians to buy a steer. The soldiers were always ready to strike a deal, especially for "booze". The Kienitzes made their alcohol from their large crop of sugar beets and it was plentiful; they purchased the steer along with five bottles of their home brew.

Alfred was not there when the large steer was captured to be brought to the Kienitz farm, but was told of the escapade. The steer was so wild when it was being apprehended it jumped over the pasture fence several times before it was detained.

Once at its new home, the steer needed to be tamed and trained to pull as a work animal. This turned out to be not an easy task. The steer was very obstinate and did not want to co-operate, even though many different avenues were attempted at calming and preparing him for assisting around the farm. The steer was extremely stubborn!

After the war, during the summer of 1945, a temporary mayor was put into position. The mayor's appointed assistant occasionally came to the Kienitzes to ask them to accommodate travellers who were on their way back home. Stopping temporarily in Pessin, these families would be people who had left their homes in East Germany during the war as the front approached. Many stayed with family in more western areas of the country.

A couple arrived one day with their horse and a two-wheeled wagon and stayed the night. Rosalie spoke freely with them, asking where they were headed. The couple had recently married, after the husband was released from a concentration camp. The Kienitzes could tell this by his appearance, as he was very thin, with a shaven head. A written paper, signed by the Russian commander, was given to this middle-aged man for his protection, so that no one had authority to take his horse or wagon.

From the first it was evident that these newlyweds were friendly, honest people. During the evening conversation, it was let known that their horse had been injured. Apparently the wagon was not properly balanced; the horse carried too much weight, which caused its skin to rub away. It was extremely infected on its back, near the mane, where the attached harness was held secure. The Kienitzes convinced the couple to rest the horse for a few days to heal the deep abrasion.

The wound was washed with a chamomile solution, as they had no medicine, but no signs of healing were noticed. The injured area was so deep one could see the bone in the lesion. In order for the horse to be back in commission, it would need extended rest.

Berlin was the couple's destination. The Kienitzes asked what they wanted to do with a horse and wagon in the city of Berlin; they would have no place to store either. Feeding the horse would also pose a problem. The Kienitz family offered to buy the horse and wagon from the couple and also drive them to the train station so they could take the train to Berlin. The couple was enormously pleased with the deal. They remained about a week before setting off for Berlin.

Several weeks later, the wound was still not completely healing. Gottlieb and Alfred developed a special harness for the horse in order to hook her up to the wagon.

Typhoid fever is a highly infectious disease which afflicted many families during that period. Four members of one family alone succumbed to the illness. The only survivors were the father and his mentally challenged daughter. His bereavement was too much to take and he turned to alcohol for comfort, eventually taking his own life. The sole surviving daughter looked after herself with the assistance of her sister-in-law.

At some point Alfred's mother contracted typhoid fever. Because they knew the doctor very well, Rosalie was allowed to stay at home during her illness; normally typhoid patients were hospitalized. The doctor was treated to an assortment of goods; the Kienitzes gave him butter, milk, eggs, meat, whatever little they had, in return for the great care he gave their family.

Rosalie was eight weeks in bed. Erna did an excellent job of caring for her mother. On a daily basis, she disinfected clothes, sheets, the entire room. She even slept in the same room as her mother. Rosalie's symptoms were horrendous, including high fever, headache, diarrhea, delirium. She lost all of her hair. The doctor visited her almost every second day. Most often Alfred picked him up from his home in Retzow. There was not much medication available in those days; it's no wonder so many died.

Neither Alfred nor any of his siblings (other than Erna) was allowed to go into Rosalie's room during that period. Standing at the bedroom door, they would talk to their mother from a distance. Erna was very strict about cleansing everything; it was a blessing and a miracle that she herself did not become ill.

After those eight weeks at home, Rosalie's condition had not improved and the doctor decided he couldn't care for her at home any longer, so he admitted her to the hospital in the city of Nauen. She remained in quarantine for another 13 weeks! The children were not allowed to visit; Gottlieb would ride with one horse and a two-wheeled wagon (the same horse and wagon they obtained from the newlywed couple) on Wednesdays and on Sundays to visit her. It was a one-hour trip one way. As Alfred needed three horses to work the fields during this busy time, on his Wednesday trip Gottlieb would ride his bike to visit Rosalie.

Once Rosalie was released, she was in amazingly good shape. Her hair grew back more beautiful than ever; she had a good appetite – which was a good thing, since she lost so much weight.

Except for Rosalie's illness, the spring and summer went smoothly, with the preparation of the fields and then planting of the beets, harvesting of the first cut of hay; summer grain was already in.

With one field of hay cut, Alfred took his ox one afternoon to make the two-kilometre trek to rake it, with the help of his two sisters. The afternoon was hot in the June sun, with the steer pulling the wagon on a slight incline on soft ground. All of a sudden, the beast decided he didn't want to pull anymore and lay down on the ground before reaching the field. Alfred hopped off the wagon and prodded the steer to get going, but you know that saying, "stubborn as an ox"; the beast was not going to budge very easily. After pushing and yelling at the animal, Alfred took the pitchfork and smacked him in the rear end, but to no avail. Extremely frustrated at the thought of the afternoon slipping away, Alfred attempted to hit the animal in the neck with the pitchfork. He became so angry at the ox for not obeying that, as he said later, "I could have shot him, only I didn't have a gun!"

Seeing that his master was not going to give up, the ox finally shook his head and rose back up on his feet. Alfred decided it was here that the ox finally respected his work more and realized who was boss. The ox understood he could not do what he pleased and was to obey the farm group from here on in. Although the large animal still tried to falter, once he was prompted what Alfred wanted, the ox reluctantly gave in.

Arriving at the field much later than they anticipated, the trio worked only for a short while, as it was milking time again for the cows. They headed back home, with no more problems from the ox, at least not on this trip.

Harvest time approached. It was around late summer to early fall when power was restored to the whole district. To save electricity, as there was not enough energy, the power was shut down for a few hours in the morning, and again in the evening. It was very frustrating for the farmers, as this was chore time in the barn. Especially as winter drew in, when daylight hours were shorter, it was complicated and very stressful to feed the animals.

With Gottlieb busy making visits to Rosalie in Nauen, it was up to Alfred, being the man of the house, to proceed with daily tasks. Christian, in his seventies by then, seldom helped around the farm.

Rye was ready to cut; the first swath was done by hand. Alfred used a scythe and went around the whole field, cutting two metres on the outer edge. His older sisters made little bundles, setting them on the outside of the field so the fifteen-year-old could proceed to harvest the grain. Because of the workload three animals, usually horses, were hooked up to the *Zugzeug* (unit for pulling) to pull the self-binder. In this case the Kienitzes' ox with his large horns was on the far left side of the *Zugzeug* (see diagraph); the two horses were hitched to the right. This self-binder cut the rye. The ox created a problem with always wanting to walk towards the uncut grain; it was very appealing to him. Alfred rigged up a mouthguard to prevent him from eating. This almost solved the problem; co-operation from the ox was slowly coming.

Zugzeug

- hook for connecting to wagon
- ← Stränge (hooked up to horse)
- ← Deixel
- Horse — Chains — Chains — Horse

The *Zugzeug* is used for all farm work: plowing, harrowing, harvesting, etc. For heavier work, the Kienitz family would hook up two horses on one side with their ox on the other side.

Chapter Seventeen

The Tractor

During the war, Gottlieb's tractor had a flat tire one day. With the fighting close to their region the Kienitz family had not had a chance to fix it before they packed up their belongings and headed south towards Alfred's Uncle Daniel's property. While they were away from their home farm a few things were pilfered, mostly by other Germans. With all the thievery that was taking place, their tractor was stolen. In early fall after the war ended, they found out from the local blacksmith that he had discovered the tractor at his shop. Gottlieb and Alfred borrowed a horse from a neighbour to add to their two horses, and headed out early one morning to Retzow to the blacksmith's business. Hitching the horses to the tractor that sported rims but no tires, Gottlieb and Alfred led the horses back home two kilometres through fields and over rough roads.

They were extremely glad to have the tractor back home again. Gottlieb was eventually able to fix it with used tires.

Later that fall, a Russian commander came and wanted to take the tractor for a while. He seemingly wanted to go on a joy ride; Alfred figured he was goofing around with nothing much else to do. The commander wanted their four-wheeled rubber wagon hooked up to the tractor. Gottlieb and Alfred grudgingly obliged. The Russians had won the war and were still showing their strong presence in the community.

Gottlieb was afraid that if the commander went for a ride in their beloved tractor, they might never see it again, so he told his teenaged son to ride along with the man. It was a nice tractor with a bench seat suitable for three riders. They were soon on their way, pulling the wagon behind them.

Alfred could not communicate much with this Russian man. He did not know where they were headed, but they ended up at the train station in a neighbouring village and came to a halt in the parking lot. The commander entered the station building with Alfred still on the tractor pondering his next move. Moments later the commander emerged with many followers. These were unfortunate folks from the Berlin area; they carried sacks and backpacks full of potatoes. With not much to eat, these destitute people were looking to trade their prized potatoes for other staples of life. Walking many kilometres to the station with their heavy load of potatoes, these citizens traded for shoes, clothes, other food … whatever they could get. Often Alfred and his family would make friends with some of these folks, allowing them to work on the Kienitz farm for the day and giving them food in return. The Kienitz family was better off than some, as they possessed livestock.

The commander directed the people towards the wagon and in a shouting manner ordered them to toss their sacks of potatoes into the back of the wagon. The people, young and old, were noticeably upset but did what they were told. Alfred was confused as to what was happening.

In the meantime, the commander jumped up onto the tractor. Alfred was ordered down to help with the handling of the potatoes. While the commander wasn't looking, Alfred threw some of the sacks back out to the people. Another man was on the wagon as well and helped with the process.

"I felt so sorry for these people," stated Alfred later, fighting back tears as he recalled the incident. "Here they were with nothing, fighting for their daily 'bread.'"

The commander and the young teen took off with the tractor and wagon in tow, full of potatoes. Alfred had no idea where their next destination was. Approaching the next village they ended up at the brewery, where the potatoes would be used to make alcohol. Unloading the haul from the wagon, the commander seemed eager at the anticipation of the schnapps that would be produced from them.

Their next destination was back at the Kienitz farm to bring the tractor and Alfred safely home.

Alfred often agonized over those poor people who were just trying to make a meagre living selling or trading their potatoes, only to have them stolen by this commander.

One day in early fall, a messenger was sent to Gottlieb with instructions that his tractor was to be used by a group of farmers from a local village for their own use. These farmers had connections with the mayor of Paulinaue and a high commander. So it was by order of the mayor and the high commander that the Kienitzes were instructed to give up their precious tractor. Gottlieb was naturally very upset, but there was nothing he could do. There were no laws governing these types of requests.

After a few days, another messenger approached with news that their tractor had blown up! The tractor was used practically day and night, most likely for plowing, and was running low on oil. When the oil was refilled, someone neglected to replace the cap. Once the tractor fired up again that evening in the darkness, no one noticed the billowing smoke that began to fill the sky. The oil spewed out and blew up the engine. Alfred figured they were either drunk or dim-witted.

Gottlieb was furious about this mishap. He enquired who was going to fix it now. No one took responsibility; so it was up to him and his son to pull the tractor six kilometres back home and make repairs to it. Not only had they lost their valuable tractor for a few days to the farmers, now it was a serious problem to get the machine working again. With virtually no tools and no mechanic, it was months before the tractor was back in commission.

Chapter Eighteen

The Helfingers

Later in the fall, around early November, the Kienitzes were again approached, this time by the mayor himself. They and another family were ordered to assist on two farms at another village for a week. The Kienitz family all pointed to Alfred to be the chosen one for this task. He was rather young to be assigned so many responsibilities, but at least he knew the other man who would be going along.

The man's last name was Helfinger (first name was uncertain, but it may have been Karl). He was about 23 years old and back home from the army. Most likely he had escaped before being taken as a prisoner of war.

So Alfred and Helfinger set off to the village of Haage with two wagons and four horses. They did not even know who was going to feed them or where they would sleep. Upon arrival in late afternoon, Helfinger was placed on one farm, Alfred on another. Their jobs would consist of plowing the fields.

Alfred slept in the restaurant, as there was no room in the farmhouse. Having brought feed from home, Alfred fed his horses and bedded them down for the night. His mother, who always looked after him well, had packed rye bread, salami and *Schmalz* (melted pork lard used for smearing on bread). She said no matter what else might happen he would have enough to eat for a while.

The following day, the farmer asked Alfred how old he was. After hearing the answer the farmer was surprised how young his helper was, and decided to plow the fields himself, using Alfred's horses and wagon.

This farmer's family of four was extremely poor. Two young boys aged ten and eight waited that night with their father and Alfred while their mother struggled to find food to put on the table. A big pile of potatoes with some gravy was placed before them. The boys, with swollen bellies, ate twice as much as Alfred. He felt so sorry for this family; they did not even own a cow. It was a tremendously difficult time for many families; for some it was a great stress just to put a meal on the table each day.

Alfred was free to do whatever he wanted while the farmer worked the fields with the Kienitz horses and wagon. He hung out in the restaurant and made eyes with the local girls. One even brought him a bouquet of wild flowers as he sat and sliced himself some salami for a rye bread sandwich.

Helfinger was not so fortunate. He worked in the fields from morning till night and did not know until heading back home that his young friend had such an easy and enjoyable time.

During the war, thieves took many items of furniture from homes where families had fled. This had happened to the Helfingers. They had five grown children; two boys did not come home from the war. The friend of Alfred's who went with him to work in the fields near Haage was their nephew.

With furniture missing at the Helfingers, they used one of the empty rooms for making music, singing and sometimes dancing. On one occasion when a group of friends gathered there, someone was hungry and suggested going for some apples. Alfred decided he would go with his friend Helfinger to get some, not saying a word to anyone else.

It didn't take them long; they were back with apples stashed in their pockets and in the fronts of their shirts. The group munched hungrily on the scrumptious fruit. One girl, Gerda Winkelhage, said, "They taste just like ours!" What Alfred and Helfinger did not tell her was that they *were* her apples, from her family's apple orchard. The young men had run to the Winkelhages' yard, two houses over, and picked the lot for their musician friends.

It was a fun and simple time to get together at these gatherings, often times with no electricity, just singing and playing music. There were usually six or eight of them, mostly all around Alfred's age.

Many evenings they would gather at the Kirschner home. The Kirschners made schnapps – only in the evening, though – by darkening the windows so no one could look in, for it was illegal to make schnapps. Mr. Kirschner, a man in his mid-fifties, would take a little of the liquor in his cup and, drinking it straight, would show the younger ones how it was done. Inhale first through the nose, take a sip, swallow, then exhale through the mouth.

In this harvest season, with winter around the corner, Gottlieb wanted to butcher one of his fine young pigs that were born earlier that year. Many laws governed the butchering of animals and it was required to obtain a permit to do this. The mayor was unaware of the Kienitz sow (one they found earlier in the year); it was livestock unaccounted for. If they butchered one of the sow's young, no one would have to know. But it would have to be done secretly.

Early one morning, water was heated in the barn (potatoes were also cooked there) to prepare for the occasion. Alfred's knowledge of butchering came in handy. Nothing was wasted; sausage was made and cooked meat was canned. The day was a success, with all members pitching in to build up the food supply for the winter.

Chapter Nineteen

More Guns ... Good and Bad

Many items and animals continued to be uncovered after the war, especially wandering horses. With many people displaced, a number of hungry animals roamed free until someone claimed them for their own, as Alfred had done with several horses and a pig.

Misplaced guns were aplenty as well.

In May of 1945, Alfred came across an MP (*Maschinenpistole*, meaning "machine pistol") army rifle in a ditch, along with a magazine of about 36 bullets. The rifle was about 50 centimetres long and could be set for automatic or semi-automatic. Along with this rifle Alfred found case housing bullets, about 500 of them. Alfred's gaze quickly scoped the landscape to make sure no one was watching when he carefully picked them up and placed them under his coat.

Extremely excited but cautious not to bring the gun and ammunition home, Alfred hid the gun in his family's own pasture field, under the grass near the fence. Owning guns was against the law at this time; no one was allowed to own one. He did tell his family about his discovery, though they were not happy about it. Especially his older sisters told him that if he was caught he would be in big trouble.

These worries meant nothing to Alfred. He was excited to own a gun and that was all that was on his mind. He loved to take the gun out secretly and go hunting. He often hid the gun in select areas of various fields.

Around November of 1945 Alfred and his father were in the field spreading manure. They had a wagon loaded full of manure and were dumping quantities of the stuff on the ground at intervals of about six metres. Using pitchforks, Gottlieb and Alfred settled into the monotonous routine of spreading the manure around. In the distance about 400 metres away, near a hayfield, was a flock of *Trappen* (similar to wild turkeys, but different in colour), numbering nearly thirty. Eyeing the birds, and knowing that his hidden gun was close by in the uncut hayfield, Alfred said to his father, "Maybe I should try to get one."

"You'd better be careful then," replied Gottlieb.

Alfred assessed the area to make sure it was safe enough to shoot one of these birds. His gaze went all around him for any movement of human beings. Leaving his pitchfork with his father, he walked downfield to retrieve the hidden gun, continuously on the alert. When he had the gun in his hands, Alfred approached a large stack of hay, planning to use it as cover. He momentarily stopped behind the hay, looking around again to make sure the coast was clear. Crouching down on his knees he began to crawl slowly closer to the birds. Between him and the flock was a ditch with a dense brush of cattails, weeds and ferns on the other side of it; he crawled further up behind the brush into the ditch. Checking the area again to make sure he wasn't being watched, he guessed the distance between him and these birds to be about 300 metres. He adjusted the settings on the gun for that distance. Lying on his abdomen he aimed and fired just once.

During the time Alfred was making his way closer to the *Trappen*, his father went about the business of spreading manure so as to not arouse any suspicion. Gottlieb, while stopping to wipe his forehead, would look often into the direction of his son, then intently to other areas, and made sure no one was watching the boy.

After Alfred fired his shot the birds took off in a scuffle. One flew up about five or six metres high before coming tumbling back down to the earth. It flapped several times and then lay still.

Alfred remained in the ditch for approximately five or ten minutes, assessing the area to make sure he was not spotted. Gottlieb continued spreading manure in a slow manner as if he were deaf to the specific gunshot, but he was looking around all the while. Leaving the gun behind in the brush, Alfred slowly approached the bird. As he bent over he picked it up by its long neck and dragged it behind him, making its presence less obvious.

Walking towards the gun, he instantly picked it up and went back to where he had hidden it in the first place. The gun was immediately concealed once again. Looking up, he walked toward his father who was standing extremely proud and shaking his head in disbelief. The pair hid the bird nearby and resumed spreading manure once again until dusk came. [Note where the bird was shot: diagram is on page 23.]

When quitting time approached the pair made sure the bird was not seen as they inconspicuously wrapped it in a long coat that Alfred had been wearing. They slipped their prize over the end of one of the pitchforks and the young marksman carried the bird home over his shoulder.

After they arrived at their household and told of the adventure to the rest of the family, Rosalie and her daughters were both excited and scared for their son and brother. They weighed the bird before plucking and found it to be nine kilograms. Another great meal!

Periodically dances were held at the local hall in the village of Pessin. One time in 1945 or 1946, on an occasion when Alfred was not present, a boy named Fritz Hermann became involved in an argument with some other boys who were taunting him. Fritz was a year younger than Alfred and he knew him quite well, as they attended the same school. The young Hermann was angry and threatened his tormentors with words of "I'll go home and get my gun if you don't quit."

When the boys heard Fritz had a gun, they revealed to others that Fritz had been bragging about the gun and threatening to use it. There were some Russian soldiers at the dance, to whom the story was relayed. The Russian soldiers took Fritz aside and questioned him. He denied owning a gun; still the Russian soldiers persisted with their query. Fritz finally admitted that he did have a gun. The soldiers led him away and no one really seemed to know what happened to him after that. Not even the uncle with whom he had lived knew of his whereabouts.

Four or five years later, Fritz Hermann re-emerged. It was revealed that he had been in Russia, but that was all Alfred heard. A few days later, Fritz escaped to West Germany, presumably to be with his parents. It was not known what his time in Russia consisted of. In all probability he spent that time in a prison camp.

Chapter Twenty

Gustav

It was quite by surprise one day when Alfred welcomed his brother Gustav back from the war.

Gustav arrived in Germany in the wee hours of the second day of January, 1946. He had travelled from Denmark to West Germany, and upon arriving at the border between East and West he was detained for interrogation. He was held at the crossing overnight until his papers were cleared. The following day, he was allowed to cross over into East Germany, where he would board a train to Nauen, arriving in that city at around 9:00 that evening. With no transportation available, he walked 16 or 17 kilometres, reaching his destination, the Kienitz homestead, at 1:00 a.m.

With the house locked up tight, Gustav proceeded to knock on the bedroom window of his parents. After three or four hard knocks Rosalie finally came to the window. She looked outside and, surprised to see her son standing there, began screaming, "Gustav, Gustav is here! Gustav is home!"

In her excitement, she forgot to let him in. Gustav had to tell her, "Go open the door!"

Gustav had a lot to tell his family about where he had been and all the things that he had endured. And his family was equally eager to tell him all they had been through. There were so many stories to tell from each side it took several weeks to hear everything.

Gustav had been sent to Denmark, where all of the young soldiers were sent for their training. One of the main reasons they were sent there was that there was ample food.

Gustav was an experienced hunter, and was quite good with a gun. In training for the war, Gustav, along with the other young men, would take practice target shots once a week. They would accumulate points for accurate gunfire and would be given the afternoon off for high points. Being the sharp-shooter he was, Gustav always earned a free afternoon and went on a shopping trip into the city. Most of his comrades were not such good marksmen. So at the beginning of the day before target practice, his comrades would already request items for Gustav to pick up for them from the city, knowing full well the sharpshooter would be released for the afternoon.

During his training the seventeen-year-old Gustav was selected to be a special sharpshooter in another region, to specialize more in his field of exper-tise. But, fortunately, he never made it to the front lines, as the war had ended just in time.

Gustav told his family that when the war was over he and his unit were all sent to the Army camp in Denmark as prisoners. A Danish farmer came along to ask the commander if any of the prisoners could repair his spinning wheel. Gustav put up his hand; the farmer brought the spinning wheel to him in prison to be restored.

After mending the wheel, Gustav wanted to test it out to see if his labour was successful. As Gustav was experienced in spinning wool, having learned the technique from his mother, he began spinning the wool still attached to the wheel. He was triumphant in his endeavours.

Upon his return, the farmer, seeing his spinning wheel repaired *and* his wool spun into yarn, was surprised, and inquired as to who had spun the wool. Gustav proudly stated that he had.

The farmer was very impressed that this young German could not only repair equipment but also spin wool into yarn. He enquired if Gustav could come to work on his farm. The proposal was accepted, and the farm was where Gustav lived for the next few weeks. He had sleeping accommodations in the house and was fed very well. The farmer and his wife treated him splendidly, just like one of their own children. Gustav felt quite at home with this family.

Gustav eventually found out what was to become of his comrades who remained at the prison camp. They were all sent to a coal mine in Belgium. Gustav was most fortunate that his mother had taught him spinning!

Near the end of his time at this Danish home, when Gustav wanted to make the journey back to his own home, the farmer advised Gustav how to go about getting home safely. The farmer even gave him a certificate to secure his safety, stating that Gustav was a relative. Gustav was also given food and money to help him survive on the way back to his home in Pessin.

Not only were the members of the Kienitz family happy to have their brother and son at home once again, it was especially beneficial to have more helping hands.

Throughout the rest of the winter and early spring everything seemed to go smoothly. Alfred, now 16, and his brother Gustav, nearly18, spent many happy moments together. Erich, their older brother, had written from France. He had become a prisoner of war in August of 1943; would they see him again? No one knew.

Chapter Twenty-one

Steer No More

Running low on meat in the spring of 1946, the Kienitz family decided it was time to butcher that stubborn ox. Needing a permit to do so, Gottlieb went to the mayor of Pessin to obtain one. They would only be allowed to keep half of the meat; the other half they would be required to give for their quota to the government. The Kienitzes planned to butcher the steer – which weighed roughly 1,000 kilograms – in their barn. For such a large animal, much assistance would be needed. So they called upon, along with Gottlieb, Gustav and Alfred, their uncle Stefan. According to the mayor, their application for a permit was in order and they could go ahead with this task.

As they wanted to catch the blood once the animal was butchered, the ox was first blindfolded. A rope was tied to his front right leg, which Uncle Stefan looked after. Gustav held the steer's head to the right. Alfred held the big axe to knock the large animal on the head. With everyone prepared, Alfred took an enormous swing; to the surprise of all of them, the ox did not fall. As the ox still stood, Alfred turned the axe around and used the sharp end this time, coming down hard. The ox still did not fall; rather, he stumbled and that caused the rope that Stefan was holding onto to break.

After a brief discussion, a decision was made to postpone the task for a while. The men reached the conclusion their efforts would have to be directed in another manner. It would take a special gun to take down this large animal.

An idea came to them!

Gottlieb rode his bike into town to the local butcher to see if he could borrow his stun gun. He arrived back home in no time at all and they began to proceed once more.

Each in his own position yet again, Alfred used the stun gun; this time the animal plunged to the ground and was ready for the next phase: catching the blood, gutting and skinning. They would allow the steer to hang for about a week.

When the meat was ready for cutting the Kienitzes completed one-half of this chore for themselves and left the other half uncut. Taking the uncut portion they drove by horse and wagon the 12 kilometres to the butcher store to deliver it. A small amount of money would be paid to them from the government for the half they had to relinquish.

Alfred took great pleasure in butchering the steer after all the hardship it had caused him, all the dreadful experiences he'd had to endure through the animal's stubbornness.

The Kienitz family was very well off again, with a good food supply. After roasting the meat and canning it, they filled their pantry for the coming months.

Alfred with horses; Rosalie and two older sisters in window.
The window is at the room in which Alfred was born.

Chapter Twenty-two

Erich

The next few months were uneventful, until June came. This is when the next surprise would emerge: Erich's arrival.

Erich was released from a prisoner camp in Cherbourg, France. When he reached the city nearest to Pessin he had to walk the 16 or 17 kilometres to their village on foot, as Gustav had done several months before, as there was no train or bus connection that day. The train only ran twice a week, Wednesdays and Saturdays.

It was Sunday morning, around eight or nine o'clock, when Erich knocked on the door of his home. No answer; he knocked harder. It was then that he noticed Erna in the kitchen, turning on her heels and heading for the basement. Erna did not recognize Erich in his uniform and thought he might have been just some soldier. At that moment, he tried the door knob; it was unlocked and he let himself in. He called out, "Now Ernashien, don't you recognize your own brother?!" (Ernashien was an affectionate name the family called her.) She stopped in her tracks and was elated that the last of her brothers had arrived home!

Alfred was in the barn doing chores when his brother Erich walked through the kitchen door. Coming into the house a short while later, Alfred had no idea his brother was already inside. Another joyful time for the family as Erich finally reached his destination. Another son and brother, home safely.

Over the next several days and weeks, Erich chronicled many of his experiences during and before his capture.

Twice during his Army tour of duty the group he was with was surrounded by enemy troops, but broke free both times. The third time they were not so successful.

It was after some heavy combat in August of 1943 that Erich and others from his unit took shelter in the basement of a house. A man out of uniform entered the basement and explained to the group of soldiers they had exactly 15 minutes to surrender or the house would be flattened. He informed them that if they surrendered no harm would come to them. With that, the stranger abruptly turned on his heels and was gone. The soldiers eyed each other in disbelief, and then their gaze fell upon their commander. The commander declared there was no other choice for them. Quickly unfastening the army belts that secured their guns and ammunition, they dropped the items to the ground. Lining up behind one another, they began the tense walk outside.

Marching outside with hands held high in the air, they were ordered to hand over personal items and all jewellery. They were marshalled into Allied Army trucks and driven to Cherbourg, a coastal town of Normandy. Once they were situated in the prison camp, it was announced over a loudspeaker, "Anyone wishing to work please raise their hands." To help pass the time, Erich quickly volunteered.

This was the beginning of an imprisonment that would last almost three years.

The prisoners were divided into groups; Erich was sent to the prison that was under U.S. conduct. He believed he was fortunate to come under the American regime, as food was extremely scarce in France. Food was in short supply even for the French guards! It was said that whatever food the American army threw away, the French guards wanted to retrieve. But the American guards would not hear of it; they did not allow the French guards to take their leftovers. The prisoners under the French regime often went hungry.

Erich told of his fellow prisoners unloading boxes of army supplies, while soldiers stood by with their guns. The prisoners carried boxes from a ship and suspected inside there were provisions of food. Two of Erich's comrades decided to break open a box to see what was inside. Erich, wanting no part of this, steered clear of their scheme.

Taking the box over to a secluded area under a railroad cart, the pair discovered salted pork was inside the box, and began to feast.

The guards, upon seeing this, forced the prisoners to eat the whole box. The duo attempted to eat what they could until they surpassed their limit.

The following day, these two prisoners, who had been so eager to know what was inside the boxes, perished. They had been poisoned from too much salt. Alfred asked his brother why they did not stop eating on their own. Erich replied, "They would have been killed."

Erich remained a prisoner when the German front pressed ahead and pushed the American front back. Becoming concerned that the Germans were advancing too quickly, the American commander brought Erich and other prisoners into his office for questioning. Extremely fearful, the commander inquired of his detainees what the intentions of the German army were, should they advance further and conquer the Americans. Although at this point Erich felt the Germans would lose the war, he really did not know what to say.

Chapter Twenty-three

The Close Call

Many more sad stories were shared. But it was time to move ahead and deal with what was happening now.

With their three sons reunited, life was a little easier on the farm for the Kienitz clan.

Gustav and Alfred were always together. They enjoyed spending their time hunting with their two mixed-breed dogs – a short female dog, named Struppi, light brown with long curly hair, and a bigger male, Tapps, with shorter, darker hair.

On a particular day in the fall of 1946 Gustav and Alfred were travelling without their dogs. They decided to take along the MP rifle that Alfred had now owned for quite some time. Leaving the village and crossing a field they approached a hill, called *Schwaberg* (this was one of two sand hills that were situated beside each other). From atop this hill they could see for many kilometres, and spotted five Russians in the distance, who were also hunting. They were about 500 metres away. Gustav and Alfred decided they should go down the hill and try to get out of sight from the other hunters. By the time they reached the bottom of the hill the soldiers were at the top of it and appeared to be looking down at the two brothers. One of these men began to approach Gustav and Alfred, who began to run in the opposite direction. They did not know at first that the Russian was following them. Looking around they noticed him catching up! What to do? Alfred raised his gun and fired a warning shot. As soon as that shot was fired, the soldier dropped to the ground to take cover. Alfred fired a second shot, after which the boys took off in haste.

As they were running Gustav yelled to his brother, "Throw that gun away, throw it away!" But Alfred refused, instead yelling back, "I won't throw the gun away 'cause this is our only protection."

The boys were clever enough not to run home. Instead they ran towards another village, the village of Retzow, in case they were still being followed. Along the way were a number of ditches and bushes, where they could move about unseen. The boys figured that if the soldiers ran after them it would be to look for them in the direction of Retzow. But when the brothers were close enough to Retzow, they doubled back and headed homeward.

On the way home Alfred hid his gun in a strawberry patch, underneath the straw.

Very cautiously the boys sneaked into their house and went up to the bedroom they shared on the second floor. From there they had an eagle's-eye view of the roads on which the soldiers might be travelling to find them. They took shelter and remained hidden for several hours, watching out the window at every moment for any army vehicles. Fortunately, nothing came of the incident. The boys were very relieved. They never said a word to anyone, not even their parents, of what had taken place, but this event made them much more cautious about their endeavours. They decided it was too dangerous to use the gun and it remained hidden in the strawberry field.

Many months later when Alfred went to look for the gun, it was gone. He assumed that one of his sisters found the gun and dropped it in one of the pasture wells, although neither Else nor Erna would admit to it. Even years later Alfred asked his sisters about the gun, and they still insisted they did not do anything to it.

Chapter Twenty-four

Suicide

Alfred's oldest sister, Erna, married Paul Gritzmacher in 1947. He was the brother of Erna's fiancé who never returned from the war. Paul and his first wife, Else, had two children, Martin and Marianne. Else took her life when the Russians invaded.

A lot of commotion happened during the time of invasion. It was reported many years later that as many as two million German women were raped by Russian soldiers.

At the height of the invasion, Else was in an area where other women were screaming, afraid of being raped. With her two young children huddling close, she reached for a butcher's knife as some Russians approached inside her home. She attempted first to take the lives of Martin, aged four, and Marianne, who was two, before taking her own. She was successful in ending her own life and also that of her son. Marianne survived. The Russian soldiers saved the little girl's life by bringing her to the hospital for emergency surgery. The medical staff "temporarily" closed her gashed wrist, but it would be years later before she had surgery again to repair the tendons properly. Alfred's sister, Erna, would raise Marianne as her own – and *only* – child.

Early in the spring of 1947 Gottlieb and Rosalie's mortgage on their home farm was coming due. In order to avoid an excessive penalty they wanted to pay the full sum, which amounted to approximately 30,000 East German marks! Knowing that their son Gustav was adept at dealings in Berlin, the couple approached him one day in March or April with an idea which to many people might seem inconceivable.

They spoke to their son about the possibility of his helping to raise the funds to pay off their mortgage. They offered Gustav anything from the farm he thought he could sell. The nineteen-year-old was excited about the challenge.

Because West Berlin was cut off from the rest of West Germany, its supplies had to be flown in. On the other hand, East Germans suffered greatly, as many essential items were not available to them. Money had little value at this time. Four East marks were equivalent to one West mark. A pair of nylons cost one hundred West marks; a broom would be the same. One single egg cost ten West marks.

Trading and bartering were the norm. Russian occupation in the eastern part of East Germany saw many soldiers trading their rationed fuel for strong alcohol. Pretty much everything was rationed at that time. Stamps were given from the government for citizens to trade them in for items including cigarettes. Non-smokers would trade their cigarettes for potatoes and peanut or rapeseed oil (which is now known as Canola oil). Rapeseed oil, or the seeds to produce it, brought in a lot of money for Gustav. Many pressed the oil secretly for their own consumption during these rationing times. Gustav wore a pouch with several pockets around his middle that contained several pounds of these seeds. This was easily hidden by wearing loose clothing when crossing the border.

Gustav became involved with the black market. The teenager arranged his schedule and charted his plan taking considerable risk and initiative. Bringing items from his parents' farmstead, he was soon travelling often between Pessin and West Berlin. The trek took just half an hour one way, so it was plausible to journey every day. He did not ask exorbitant prices and knew he was assisting the West German people, as there were some items they had no access to.

A staple of life, food was something easy for Gustav to get his hands on and sell. He brought butter and eggs from the farm into West Berlin under the pretense the eggs were to be hatched. This was close to Easter, so it was not a problem to smuggle the eggs across the border. Befriending the Russian soldiers, he swapped them strong homemade alcohol in exchange for the Russians' gasoline, which he then brought back home, as the Kienitzes needed fuel to run their motorcycles. Gustav also had Alfred butcher a beef and with the help of some Russians the older son brought the meat across the border. The young entrepreneur had a distributor lined up to sell the beef, and sold as much as he could. His parents were not being purely selfish, as they were helping the people of West Berlin. It was a win/win situation. In just under a month, after taking great risk Gustav had raised the 30,000 marks needed to pay off the mortgage!

Chapter Twenty-five

Hunting With Knives

In the autumn of 1947 Gustav and Alfred again decided to go hunting, this time with their dogs and without a gun. A neighbour lad of about 14 years of age liked to hang around the older boys. Zemke was his last name and one day he went along on the hunt.

The boys headed to an area that was covered by marshland, where there were many sections that contained dips in the land. Long ago, the moss-type substance that grew in that area was cut, left to dry and made into large brick-shaped material which was later used to heat homes. These brick-like objects were known as *Torf*.

The area was covered with bulrushes and different types of grasses, many of them grown very high. In the dips the ground remained water-filled from morning to evening while the ridges remained dry; it was a good area for wild boars to hide and make their home.

Gustav and Alfred decided to split up. Gustav would take Zemke and the two dogs and head in one direction, Alfred headed in another. Both brothers were armed with sharp knives. Not long after they split up, as Gustav and Zemke walked towards the high grass one dog began barking. The noise chased out seven wild boars towards the pasture where Alfred was. The boars ran in different directions, with the dogs close behind, nipping the boars in the rear. One boar became confused in the scuffle and decided to head back into the high grass with the small dog chasing him.

Standing in the lofty grass about 10 metres away, Gustav held his knife ready for action as the boar approached with the barking dogs behind. To his surprise the boar attacked him; Gustav grabbed the boar by the ears and held on tight. Grasping the boar with both hands and thus unable to use his knife, he yelled to Alfred, "Hurry, come over here!"

Alfred yelled back, "The water is so high!"

"Never mind the water, just get over here!"

So, although he was getting drenched, Alfred ran through the wet land towards his brother. He grabbed one leg of the boar and threw it to the ground, using his knife to kill the wild pig. It all happened so quickly. The boys were mighty proud of their catch.

In all the excitement they had forgotten about their little friend, Zemke. They began calling to him with no response. They shouted some more for him and searched the area, but there was no finding the young boy. Alfred and Gustav heard the next day that Zemke was so frightened with all the squealing and yelling that he ran home as fast as his legs could carry him! The boys roared with laughter as they pictured their young friend fearfully running away from the commotion.

The brothers pulled the boar to the edge of the high grass and covered it. At this time the larger dog appeared. In a hurry to get home to retrieve transportation to haul their boar, the boys ran as fast as they could with their dogs. When they arrived home, no time was wasted; they hooked up the horse to the two-wheeled wagon. Just then their father appeared.

"What did you want to do?" Gottlieb inquired, a bit baffled by their speed.

The boys proudly told their dad they needed to go pick up a wild boar.

"*What* did you do?!" asked Gottlieb in disbelief.

"Dad, we just killed a wild boar; we have to go" came the quick reply.

Their father was shocked.

The boys got on the wagon and made haste towards their waiting game. Not long afterward they returned with the boar, carefully covering him so no one could see their bundle in the wagon. They placed him in the barn and readied him for the next process; the young boar weighed 40 kilograms.

They decided to sell half of the boar in Berlin. Gustav was an expert in this area and knew it would fetch a good price. He and Alfred split the money and their family benefited from the other half of the boar. They also presented a roast to Zemke's family, who were extremely poor. It was a favourable situation for all.

Because of Alfred and Gustav's keen hunting skills, their large family did not go hungry too often.

Chapter Twenty-six

Alfred Obtains His Licence and Meets Margot

During and after the war meat was very scarce, as there was not enough livestock. So when Gustav and Alfred were able to find the wild boar, or when Alfred shot the *Trappe*, it was like a Christmas meal in the making.

In the spring of 1948, Gottlieb spoke to his son about obtaining his butcher's certificate. Alfred had already completed one year and was required to finish his apprenticeship before being licensed. Alfred's father approached his old boss, Otto, to see if he could resume his education. Otto agreed, although there was not really much work at the time as there was still a shortage of meat.

Alfred would travel to Otto's place of business and stay overnight for a few days at a time. The extent of the business was then mainly rabbits. Butchering sometimes dozens of rabbits a week, they also made sausage. It was a very poor era. After the war customers bought their meat using food stamps; they were only allowed a certain quota per person. Men who worked hard received more food stamps than the average person; children received far fewer. On pieces of paper from the government would be documented food stamp information of how much each person was allowed. A few nights a week, Otto would glue the food stamps onto newspaper and send them in to the government. In return Otto would receive more meat from the food supplier. Everything was regulated. If 100 kilograms of meat was given to Otto, he would have to show 100 kilograms worth of food stamps for it.

Otto's shop was open for business from Monday to Saturday. Every Tuesday morning, pork would be cooked for sausage. The townsfolk all knew that Otto would have produced "broth" from the cooked pork. The lineups were quite long on Tuesdays as people waited for the delicious broth, from which they could make their own soups. Broth was not regulated by the government, and was sold for a very reasonable price.

As time went on, livestock became slightly more abundant; Otto and his assistants began butchering more hogs and beef. After receiving his certificate in the spring of 1950, Alfred remained friends with Otto and his son.

Alfred had joined the volunteer fire department in Pessin. In the fall of 1948 he and his young firefighting colleagues, along with a couple of others, decided to put on a comedy skit called "Where is it burning?" One of the actors, after learning his lines, moved away, so another had to step in to take his place. As the novice was not familiar with his lines, Alfred would whisper the words to him, feeding him each successive line, to the great amusement of the audience. The play was such a success that they took the show on the road to Retzow and Rebbik.

Along with "Where is it burning?" the boys put on a skit about a lion tamer. A man would come out on stage and ask if anyone knew how to tame lions. From among the group of boys on stage, Alfred would raise his hand up high and yell with enthusiasm, "Me!" Alfred and the others would leave the stage; the audience would hear lions roaring and someone screaming for help. Next Alfred would appear on stage quite frightened, running in his underwear and with scratched legs. The audience went wild with laughter.

Helmut Krinke was one of Alfred's best friends. Helmut was also in the play. He was the boyfriend of Ursula Krueger, who lived in Retzow.

When the show went to Retzow, Ursula was in the audience with her younger sister, Margot. They both laughed hysterically. When she saw Alfred appear on stage in his torn underwear during the skit, Margot recalled, "I laughed my head off."

Once the show was over the lights would dim and dancing would begin. Helmut introduced Alfred to Margot and Alfred asked her to dance. They seemed to hit it off and began dating.

Luise went to High School in West Berlin from 1949 – 1952, coming home every weekend by train to her parents home. As a hungry young girl, she looked forward to her mother's meals. After finishing school in March of '52, Luise went to Braunschweig, which at that time was the British Sector, where Gustav lived. Her brother found a rare opportunity for employment for Luise.

Margot lived with Ursula, their younger sister, Ilse, and their parents, Erna and Georg.

It was also this year that Alfred's sister, Erna, married and left for West Berlin, as they saw their future not under the influence of the communist party.

In 1949 or 1950, while at Otto's butcher shop a repairman was summoned to repair Otto's walk-in cooler. On one of his visits back home, Alfred retold the story of the repairman while his mother listened with great interest. As her eyes widened, she asked her son if he could talk to this man about getting them a refrigerator. The repairman was due back again to finish up his maintenance job and Alfred seized the opportunity to make his inquiry for his mother. A week later, the repairman contacted Alfred to let him know he had a used unit. It was carried in a side car of a motorcycle with Alfred riding along with the repairman! It was the very first refrigerator in the town of Pessin and the Kienitz owned it.

Margot with sister Ursula, their father and horses in 1940.

Margot with her older sister Ursula and parents, Georg and Erna in 1940

Margot with younger sister Ilse, 1942

Margot with Ilse in 1946, with their mother in background, at their home in Retzow

Margot in her backyard; around the age of sixteen

Chapter Twenty-seven

Love Blooms

With his butcher papers to his credit, Alfred remained at home and farmed with his father and brothers. During the winter months, Alfred would visit the area farmers and butcher pigs right on their farms; this also included making sausage for some of them. He made a good extra income and was able to watch his savings grow. He dreamed of someday being his own boss as a butcher or farmer.

In 1948 Gustav left home and went to live in West Germany. Gustav's heart was not into farming. He preferred to work in his own trade of making fine-optic glasses. Gustav eventually applied to emigrate to Canada, and his application was successful in 1953; before that time, because of Hitler and the war, no Germans were allowed into Canada.

Alfred and Margot's relationship blossomed. Two or three evenings a week he would go to visit her in Retzow. Margot had a busy life helping her father on the farm. Since there were no sons for Georg and Erna (an infant son died after Margot) it would be the eldest daughter who would have to help with farm duties. Ursula had trouble with her bladder, which kept her close to home helping her mother. Ilse was seven years younger than Margot. So it was up to Margot to help with farm chores, which included tending to the livestock – pigs, dairy cows, and chickens. It was a mixed farming operation like most farms at that time. There were many days spent in the field doing hard heavy labour. She was always heard saying that she would *never* marry a farmer.

Since Ursula's boyfriend, Horst, was the only son in his family, his parents would hand their farm down to him. As Margot worked very hard for many years on her family's farm, her parents' wish was that some day they would be able to give that farm to her and her husband.

Margot and Alfred fell in love and continued to see each other often, even though he was a farmer. She was very beautiful, with wavy brown hair, and soft-spoken, while he was comical and outspoken, with a quick temper. Both were hard-working and eager to make a decent living. They had talked of marriage during their courtship, but when Margot became pregnant it was natural that they should marry sooner. On August 12, 1951, Alfred and Margot became engaged.

Chapter Twenty-eight

The Wedding

The couple married on November 2, 1951. Gustav was happily able to make it from the West (Berlin) for his brother's wedding.

Polterabend takes place on the night before a wedding in Germany. *Polterabend* means 'eve-of-the-wedding party'. It is similar to shivaree in the Western world. In the afternoon before this farewell party starts, most of the friends and neighbours come along to decorate the entrance of the bride's house with flowers; they do this in absence of the couple.

During the afternoon of November 1, young children appeared at Margot Krueger's home and threw old cracked dishes in front of the main door, smashing them to the ground. (Glass is not used, as it might bring mishap.) These dishes would have had chips or cracks in them and would have been previously set aside especially for the next upcoming wedding.

After the children throw dishes at a *Polterabend* the bride emerges with cake while the groom looks after the soft drinks. After mingling outside for a while, the children eventually leave and later the adults go through a similar ritual.

Most of the friends and neighbours bring along something rotten or used china and earthenware. They throw all this to the ground outside the house to make fragments (*poltern* means "crash about"). This shall bring luck to the couple in the future and it signifies that their childhood is gone. So this party is the farewell to yesterday while the wedding day is the beginning of the future. The *Polterabend* tradition continues today in many areas of Germany.

As well as delicious homemade cakes, open-faced rye bread sandwiches are served to the adults, and beer or schnapps are offered instead of soft drinks.

While socializing in the yard, friends tell stories about the engaged couple, mainly stories of a funny and personal nature. Friends who stay too long at this farewell party sometimes fall asleep the next day at the wedding ceremony!

Cleaning up the broken dishes and throwing waste into the garbage is the bride and groom's task the following morning. After doing their cleaning-up on the morning of November 2, Alfred and Margot went by horse and buggy to the government marriage bureau, which is called *Standesamt*, to sign their marriage papers.

Most wedding ceremonies take place at two o'clock in the afternoon at a local church. This wedding was to take place at the Lutheran church in Retzow. Guests and the wedding party arrived at the home of the bride around one o'clock. With the flower girl walking in front, they processed about 500 metres to the church, where the pastor awaited them. Margot's sister, Ilse, who was eleven years old, was the flower girl.

As was customary, the church bells began to chime as the wedding group walked along, and continued ringing until they arrived at the church and entered it. The guests seated themselves. After the ceremony, the guests, again in accordance with tradition, formed a procession behind the bride and groom and walked to where the reception was to be held, a hall two doors down from where the Kruegers lived.

The Wedding March

Behind Isle (Margot's sister) and Marianne (the stepdaughter of Alfred's sister) were Margot and Alfred followed by Helga (Margot's Tante Herta's stepdaughter); Ursula and Horst; Herta and Oskar (Margot's aunt & uncle); Ruth (Margot's cousin) and Gustav. Friends and family filled the gap between the wedding couple and their parents, who brought up the rear.

After pictures the party began with a meal. At the head table the bride's parents sat beside Alfred and the groom's parents sat beside Margot. (The best man and maid of honour did not exist in this German tradition.)

About 75 guests danced and had a marvellous time. The party lasted until the wee hours of the morning. Alfred and Margot, as was tradition, said goodbye to the last of their guests around 7:00 a.m. on Saturday morning.

The wedding took place on a Friday so that Alfred and Margot would have one extra day after they married before they had to head back to work. But their leisure time was cut short in order to ship potatoes for the following Monday. After a brief nap in the morning, Saturday afternoon was spent sorting potatoes. Sunday afternoon was reserved for acquaintances to stop by for cake and coffee and to wish the new couple well.

As a wedding gift Alfred's parents gave them two milking cows, 15 chickens and two sheep.

Alfred moved in with Margot, her parents and her younger sister, Ilse and older sister Ursula (Horst Preubisch married Ursula on May 5, the following year). With the newlywed couple and Margot's parents both in a position of lacking funds, times were tough.

Erna, Margot's mother, was a wonderful person with a big heart, working hard and never complaining; she was always pleasing her family. Erna was a great cook and passed this knowledge on to her daughters – although with Margot doing much of the outside work with her father, she did not learn many of the cooking skills until she started her own family. Georg, on the other hand, was a little more difficult to get along with. He and Alfred had a few clashes regarding the farming process. Alfred was a high achiever and it seemed to him that staying on his in-laws' farm (in order to take it over eventually) would not be successful.

Chapter Twenty-nine

The Babies Are Born

One February evening Margot went into labour and told Alfred to fetch the midwife, who lived 10 kilometres away. The midwife knew roughly when Margot's due date was. There was no telephone, so Alfred sped off on his motorcycle. Arriving at the midwife's residence around 10:00 p.m. he discovered she was not at home. Upon inquiry of the neighbours, it was revealed she was out dancing. Driving to the dance hall not far away, Alfred put an abrupt end to her fun evening. The annoyed midwife travelled home on the back of Alfred's motorcycle to obtain her medical bag, then they zoomed on to Retzow. They reached the Kruegers' house around midnight. Keeping Margot company in Alfred's absence was her kind mother Erna.

The midwife, feeling the effects of the late evening and a few drinks, was very sleepy. The labour progressed with no signs of an immediate delivery. Erna boiled water to make coffee to keep the midwife awake, but she had a few snoozes anyway. The midwife was a little cross with the family for calling her so soon.

The following day was Monday, February 25, 1952. At 8:00 a.m. Alfred's and Margot's first child was born, Anneliese Margot Marlies. Alfred's older sisters suggested calling the baby girl Marlies, but Margot identified that name with a snotty-nosed child in their village and would not hear of it. She satisfied her sisters-in-law by adding it as a middle name instead.

Alfred and his father-in-law were in the yard chopping wood to pass the time when someone came running out to let them know the great event had finally taken place.

Seeing no future in store for his young family, since his farming ideas were so different from those of his father-in-law, Alfred decided to talk to his father about moving back to Pessin. There was a house around the corner from Gottlieb and Rosalie where an older couple with the last name of Kressin lived. After speaking with the couple they agreed to sell the house to Margot and Alfred, with his parents help, and with conditions from the Kressins. The older couple would be allowed to live with Alfred and Margot there until one of them passed away; at that time, the remaining living spouse would move out. Another older couple lived upstairs and would continue to rent that space. After some minor renovations to the downstairs, Alfred and Margot moved to their first home in the fall of 1952, a house with about 3.6 hectares (9 acres) of land. As it turned out, Herr Kressin passed away in August the following year; his wife would go to live with a daughter who also lived in Pessin.

In 1953 Alfred received a surprise phone call from his former boss, Otto, who informed him about a butcher shop with a farm that was available in the town of Kotzen – which, oddly, means "Vomit". (Yes, I know, it's hilarious; I can hardly stop laughing just writing it. Can you imagine the conversation? Where do you live? Oh, I live in Vomit.) Kotzen was 15 kilometres from Pessin and 17 from Retzow.

After viewing the property, the young family decided it was a good idea; they would rent it for two years to see how things went. At the end of the two years they would have the option of buying the property. Sister Else occupied Alfred and Margot's home for the period of the lease and maintained the grounds. This was another tremendous moment in their lives. On the first day of November that year they moved to their new home in Kotzen to begin their own business. Margot was pregnant and in her last trimester with their second child.

Twenty-eight days later, Margot began having labour pains. Because the butcher shop was attached to the home, a blanket was hung in the doorway to separate home and store and to try to muffle the sounds of the activities in the busy shop. A woman in labour does not fancy the smell of sausage or fresh meat!

It was a different midwife this time, but, like the first one, she also became upset at the Kienitzes. Not because she was called too early, but because she could have been called much sooner. She was picked up and brought by tractor to their home, and barely an hour later – on the twenty-eighth day of November, 1953 – their second child was born, Manfred Alfred. Manfred's midwife, unlike the first one, was a wonderful, caring woman. Alfred's reason for not bringing her earlier was that the first midwife had said she was called much too soon and he was afraid this one also would have to wait too long.

Just getting used to a newborn and with a toddler in tow, Margot became pregnant again. Still assisting Alfred with the business, Margot did her best to keep up in the shop as well as tending to the children and house. The due date was supposed to be sometime in March of 1955, but on January 25 she surprisingly gave birth to twins, both girls. It was a tragic premature birth; Margot was helping with the work of the butcher business when she began to bleed one day after a heavy workload. She was taken to the hospital, where she gave birth to the girls. One weighed 900 grams (2 pounds), the other 1,180 grams (2.6 pounds); one girl lived only a couple of hours, the other died the following day. Alfred's eyes never gazed upon them, as the hospital officials baptized them right away before placing them in two small caskets. They were named Margitt and Margrit. Had they lived, their parents would have chosen different names. These two baby girls grew in the same womb and were placed in the same grave together. Their similar names reflected the intimacy they shared during their brief life.

It was an extremely sad occasion but there was little time to grieve in the midst of a demanding establishment and two small children at home. Showing emotions illustrated weakness and this was simply not permitted back then. A small funeral was held a few days later with a few close family members in attendance.

The twins' grave. The wooden frame bordering the grave was filled with pebbles in order to keep the weeds down. When Alfred paid a visit to Germany in fall of 2008, the graves had been demolished. If a grave is not kept up and dues are not paid, the law states that the grave will be demolished to make room for new ones.

Opel P4, approximately 1934 model. It was a four-seater vehicle that was converted into a two-seater with a box in the back for transporting meat and small livestock. It was purchased when the Kienitzes moved to Kotzen.

As it turned out, the butcher shop business was extremely hard work and not very lucrative, for many citizens used food stamps to buy meat. Alfred's mother was very displeased with their initial decision to rent the shop and felt greatly relieved when the two years were up. At that time Alfred and Margot moved back to Pessin, to their former home. Two more boys were born during this time; Berndt on July 16, 1956 and Wolfgang a year later on August 28, 1957.

Also in 1956, Alfred's sister, Else, left Pessin for West Berlin with her new husband.

Chapter Thirty

The Hunting Licence

In Pessin, Alfred drove a tractor in the warm seasons for the farmers' co-op operated by the government; in the winter he travelled to various farms and did butchering for them.

Starting in 1954 Alfred belonged to the government-owned hunting agency, which meant he was allowed to hunt at certain times with a police escort and government-owned gun. Alfred exchanged sausage with one of his pals in order to gain entry to this organization, of which his brother Erich was also a member. To be privileged for this, one was required to become a police helper, to accompany officers on various duties; it was also obligatory to inform the police of any wrongdoing in the community. Alfred, along with Erich, kept a low profile on this, as they did not want to 'tattle' on their neighbours and friends.

It was necessary for hunters to renew their hunting licences yearly. Monthly meetings were ongoing for them as well. One meeting in 1958, at which individuals were to collect their renewed licences, was troubling for the brothers. After almost everyone had received a licence, except Erich and Alfred, the instructor advised Erich in confidence that he wanted to speak to him outside.

As soon as they were in private, the instructor reported to Erich he would give his licence back to him if Erich joined the organization of the government farmers (*Landwirtschaftliche Produktionsgenossenschaft*, or LPG for short). In this organization, farmers are required to give up ownership of their land, as well as to pay an amount per hectare that had been owned, to the organization. The LPG did not want money; instead they wanted livestock or good machinery. Erich flatly rejected the offer. He simply stated he would rather give up his licence and remain a private farmer.

Next it was Alfred's turn to exit with the instructor for a discussion about his licence. Choosing his words very carefully, the instructor told Alfred there was an incident that had to be investigated before Alfred would receive renewal of his hunting privileges. He said he would be notified of this shortly.

A few days later the local policeman, Hans Heustetter, who trusted Alfred, came and spoke to him in confidence. A certain individual had reported to the police that Alfred had purchased young livestock for butchering. Butchering was not allowed unless it was reported and followed legal procedures. Several times Alfred had tricked the meat inspector to make him think he was cutting up a bull calf instead of a female. Certain organs had been 'transplanted' and were missing.

Alfred got himself out of hot water very easily by explaining to the officer that he did not buy the calves from the farmers. He only butchered the animals and sold the meat for the farmers; in return, they paid Alfred for his labour. The officer, listening intently, instantly agreed with Alfred, and asserted certainty that Alfred would never conduct such illegal business.

To make sure they would verify his story, Alfred immediately visited his farm neighbours to let them know what he had told the officer, just so they would be able to say the same thing if asked. Alfred would have required a licence to buy livestock from farmers, so he wanted to make sure they would cover for him – and they did.

A few days later, Alfred got his hunting licence back. What a man will do to hunt!

In that same year, Alfred took a course to become an artificial insemination technician.

In the fall of 1958 or 1959. A stranger takes a photo of Alfred just after he picked up the motorcycle that the company supplied him with. He worked for a cattle breeding station performing odd jobs, and became acquainted with all the animals. After attending a school for six weeks he became a licensed artificial inseminator. Once licensed, Alfred had his own district that included 3,500 cows that he maintained.

Margot with her young brood in 1959 on a visit to
West Germany to visit Alfred's family

Chapter Thirty-one

Assisting Escapees

Police officer Hans Heustetter came to talk to Alfred on another occasion, this time to talk confidentially about Inge Gossman and Erich Henschke. He found Alfred in the yard of Gottlieb and Rosalie's house, where the pair talked in private.

It seems that a couple, Inge and Erich who were engaged, were in question from the police. Erich had escaped from East Germany a few years earlier and maintained a business in West Berlin. Inge lived there as well, however her parents lived in Pessin and she travelled frequently to and fro.

The officer probed Alfred, "You know Inge Gossman pretty good."

"Yes," replied Alfred cautiously. "We went to school together." Alfred had also gone to school with her brothers, some of whom were close to Alfred's age.

"Maybe you can find out when she is coming home from her brother's (place) because we want to arrest her."

When he heard these words, it was as though lightning had struck Alfred in the heart. "Yes," he said, "I know her pretty good, okay. I will find out."

Alfred's mind then began working on how he might save Inge.

He usually drove with motorcycle by her parents' home twice a day on his way to and from farm duties as artificial inseminator. The day after his conversation with the police officer, he noticed Fritz, one of Inge's brothers, outside working close to the road. Alfred stopped his motorcycle and talked casually with him. He asked how Inge was doing and when was the next time she would be coming to Pessin.

Fritz answered she was anticipated home that weekend.

Alfred told of his conversation with the officer and stated firmly, "Please tell her not to come."

Fritz did not take this so seriously, and did not inform Inge prior to her visit. It was not until she arrived at her parents' home that he relayed the news of her impending arrest.

She was shocked and became so frightened that she left immediately, not taking anything that would hinder her return. Rather than going by her normal route, Fritz led her by a different path to another train station. The train from this station had to make two stops before crossing the border. Inge said goodbye to her brother and boarded anxiously, but without incident.

The next stop was Brieselang. There was an exchange of passengers there, after which the train began moving on to the last stop before the border.

At the last stop, Falkensee, police would routinely check passengers and their passports. This stop would take several minutes longer than stops at other train stations. Inge knew this and was prepared to show her passport. To her distress the officer requested for her to follow him to the control office for search. She was devastated, and presumed this was the end but still tried to show little emotion. She thought they had discovered her and she would now be captured!

Her baggage was searched intensely. It was her good fortune and intelligent thinking that she had not taken any food or articles that were not allowed for border crossing. She was quite ecstatic and relieved when the officers dismissed her back to the train. This had just been a random routine check and she was now on her way back to her home in West Berlin.

After this harrowing experience she made no further visits to East Germany. Inge had an interesting story to relay to her fiancé, but he agreed that it was too risky for her to try to get back to see her family again. It wasn't until after the wall came down some 30 years later, in 1989, that she would finally set foot in her homeland once again! She and Erich reckoned they would marry in West Berlin without the presence of their families, since it would be too dangerous for family members to attend their special event.

Once he heard news from her brother that Inge was safe, Alfred felt a great relief. He knew he had made a wise decision to inform Inge's family of the threat to her freedom. The police officer never found out that Alfred warned Inge about their impending arrest for her.

Over a period of about five or six years, Alfred contributed to the escapes of a number of people fleeing East Germany. These escapes always took place in the dark on back/side roads. Around 1954, before Inge took flight for good, he assisted a family escape while he and Margot were still living in Kotzen.

Alfred butchered a pig for this family and in consequence became good friends with them, developing a great mutual trust. The lady of the house told Alfred she and her family would like to leave the country, and asked Alfred if he could be of assistance to their plan. He was quite willing; he always felt inclined to help others where he could. Alfred knew that his home country was very much under communist rule and many people wanted to break free of that.

After discussions as to what the couple, who were in their mid-fifties, had in mind about the escape, it was determined one cow and two beautiful horses would need to be sold. Wanting to keep everything low-key so as not to alert neighbours, friends, or any government officials, Alfred and his friends realized the sale would have to be carried out only a day or two before the day of the escape. It would be best to transact the sale under cover of darkness.

The task at hand necessitated great secrecy. Only a handful of people could be trusted. Obviously the couple felt they could trust Alfred. If he had turned out to be the police informant that he was supposed to be, the couple would have been put in jail. There was a law that if you attempted to flee or assist in another's getaway, the minimum penalty was a two-year jail term. By helping these people, Alfred was taking an immense risk.

Alfred proceeded with utmost caution. Only closely-trusted citizens would be given an opportunity to purchase the animals; no advertisement of any kind was made known to the general public. Alfred lined up a buyer (Alfred's Uncle Daniel) for the horses plus a wagon. The evening that the couple was to leave for West Germany, Alfred drove the horses and wagon to his farm. The buyer came that same evening to Alfred's home, then left for his two-hour excursion home using a lantern. He had paid Alfred the previous day. After the horses were in the buyer's possession, the woman came to Alfred to collect her money. The milking cow was purchased by Alfred himself, and turned out to be a good cow.

This cow had her own escape story. Grazing in the pasture one day, she decided to make a run for her old home. Alfred had to retrieve her while other neighbours were laughing, as they knew where her previous home was.

Escaping proved much easier for the couple than for their cow; they, fortunately, were not brought back to *their* home.

More Escapes

Alfred had a good friend, Klaus Thiel, who lived in Senske about three kilometres away. Klaus's mother-in-law wanted to flee the country, as she did not see a future where she was. A few relatives in West Germany would be anticipating her arrival. She owned a milking cow which Alfred purchased from her for a fair price.

Klaus and Alfred went over to Klaus's mother-in-law's house one evening and led her milking cow by a rope along back roads to Alfred's parents' farm. Walking beside the railway tracks, Alfred and Klaus came upon a section lit up at a crossroad. Klaus went ahead to check to see if the coast was clear in the lighted area, while Alfred stayed in the shadows waiting for the go-ahead. As soon as Klaus signalled to him, Alfred quickly led the cow past the illumination and on into the darkness once again. Rosalie and Gottlieb's farm was not far off now; this would be the new home for the cow, as Alfred's barn was full. Klaus's mother-in-law made her way into West Germany without incident.

On another occasion, a farmer from Retzow enlisted Alfred's aid to sell two of his milking cows to Alfred's parents. This was easily accomplished one evening, as the Kienitzes' pasture was near the farmer's pasture. The farmer and his wife, along with their younger children, escaped with no obstruction.

Another instance involved Reinhold Hermann, a Pessin resident. Alfred bought a milking cow from Reinhold. Through the darkness of night Alfred led the cow over the fields to his property. Reinhold had other livestock that he just left behind when he took off for a new life in West Berlin.

Chapter Thirty-two

The Kienitzes' Escape Unfolds

By the early spring of 1960, the government was putting pressure on the farmers to join the LPG. Upon joining this group, farmers would not be their own bosses anymore; they would pay to the LPG a sum per hectare of the land they had owned. But the LPG did not want these sums in cash; rather, they stipulated that livestock or high-quality equipment be given. Farmers would work for minimum wages for the LPG. To hard-working farmers this was disgraceful! They and their ancestors had toiled their land for generations, through many hardships, only to be forced to succumb to the dictates of the government-owned *Landwirtschaftliche Produktionsgenossenschaft*.

Among the farmers who resisted joining were Alfred's brother Erich and their father. Gottlieb and Erich farmed 18 hectares. The LPG existed for many years; for the non-ambitious farmer it was not a bad deal, but for the hardworking grower/livestock producers, it would not allow for expansion on their farms. Joining the LPG took away the farmer's freedom and rights. Gottlieb and Erich were highly motivated and worked well together. Alfred was happy not to be a farmer at this time, working instead as an artificial insemination technician.

A deadline was set for all farmers to join; the date was sometime in April of 1960. A convoy of cars drove through the streets of Pessin; from these vehicles, loudspeakers blared a message to the community to encourage all to join the LPG. For any farmer who had not yet joined, the entourage would stop in front of his property and yell and ridicule to inform the public that this particular farmer was against the LPG and supported the West instead.

A few days later an evening meeting was scheduled in the town for farmers to attend and become members of the LPG. This was the breaking point for Gottlieb, Rosalie, and Erich and his wife, Margot, and their twins, Klaus and Christiane (pronounced Christiana), who were eight years old at the time. They had been preparing for several months to escape to the West, having anticipated the LPG's pressure. All their detailed planning would be soon set in motion.

Life under the communist system was becoming worse in general, with people losing their freedom. There were between 1,000 and 3,000 people *daily* who left East Germany in search of a better, freer life. This was reported on the West German radio station. The East Germans listened to this station against the will of their government. The authorities would send spies to investigate who was listening to what on the radio; children would be asked in school what station their parents were tuning in to.

For safety reasons, the Kienitz family planned to split up and take separate escape routes, at different times. Alfred and his wife Margot knew about their family's plot six months in advance, and kept it secret.

The day that the escape began was March 14, 1960. That morning, Erich's wife Margot, along with her twin children, pedalled their bikes to Retzow, to the home of Erna and Georg Krueger. As in all small towns, people all knew of one another. Erich and Margot knew the parents of Alfred's wife (who was also named Margot), and at their home is where the bicycles were left (although the Kruegers likely had no knowledge of the planned escape). Erich's Margot and the twins then walked to the bus station and took a bus to the city of Nauen. (The trio left by bus from Retzow because they were not well known there. Had they got on the bus in their own town, it would have raised suspicion.)

Riding along on the bus, Margot was surprised to discover that its next stop was in Pessin, her hometown! Holding her breath she waited for passengers to get on, keeping her head low and her children obstructed from the new travellers boarding. Luckily, no one recognized her, and the bus travelled on to Nauen, where Margot and the twins boarded a train to Berlin.

"Where are we going?" the inquisitive children enquired.

"To Alexanderplatz, to buy something," came Margot's reply nonchalantly.

The children grew excited about such a shopping excursion. Margot did not want to tell the curious children their plan. Not yet.

After Nauen came two more stops in East Germany before they would arrive in Berlin-Spandau Station, where they would exit and be safe. They took no belongings with them that would give them away.

As they departed from the train station in Berlin, Margot, Klaus and Christiane walked towards the house of Erich's sister (Erna), which was half an hour away. The children were surprised to be heading in the direction away from Alexanderplatz. It was then that their mother explained with watery eyes that they would not be going back. Step one of the plan had been successfully executed.

By lunchtime that same day, Gottlieb and Rosalie were ready to implement their part of the scheme. Walking from their home to the Pessin bus station, they boarded a bus that would drive them to Nauen. From Nauen they took the same route as their daughter-in-law and grandchildren had done earlier in the day. As they took absolutely no personal belongings, the authorities at the border would presume the elderly couple were taking a day trip. By supper the grandparents were reunited with their family at the home of Erna, their daughter.

Erich was arranging last-minute details before his departure. It was getting dark and he was anxious to tie up loose ends. That was the evening the LPG was holding its meeting. Half an hour before the meeting, an LPG officer arrived to make sure Erich would be there to sign papers and join. This officer encountered Alfred, who was there to move a refrigerator with the help of a friend, Siegfried Graewe (pronounced Graiva). The two hesitated when the officer asked for Erich.

"In the house," Alfred answered.

The officer found Erich inside the house and asked if he was still planning to attend the meeting.

"Yes, I'll be there, I just want to have a bite to eat," replied Erich. This satisfied the officer, and off he went.

Once Erich had left for the meeting, Alfred and his friend took the fridge to a neighbour's barn, which would later be moved to Alfred's home, to store for a few days till the dust settled. Alfred also removed a few small memorable items from his parents' house and waited patiently for his brother's return.

Shortly before 11:00 p.m., Erich arrived back home from his meeting. Not wasting any time, he and Alfred departed in Alfred's car for the village of Staaken, where Erich would be allowed to walk over the border into West Germany. Staaken was the last village along the route.

As they drove, Erich related his story of the LPG meeting. Along with the mayor, there were big shots present from the Communist party. They demanded every farmer join the LPG. Erich requested 24 hours to contemplate signing his land over to the group. They accepted this under one condition: that he sign a piece of paper saying that when he came back, he would be willing to sign of his own free will. The Communists wanted to report to the government that Pessin, by the next evening, would be one hundred percent socialist. This would set an example for the rest of the country that others would follow and also sign their land over. The mayor and the Communists, shaking hands with Erich, were satisfied with this arrangement and allowed him to have his 24 hours of "thinking time".

When the brothers arrived in Staaken at 11:30 that evening, passports would need to be seen by border patrol, which consisted of two armed German police officers and two Russian soldiers, also armed.

Alfred parked his car, fought back the tears as he hugged his brother and watched as Erich proceeded towards the patrol station. He lost sight of him for a while in the crossing area. Then as Erich departed, he walked up a flight of 25 steps onto a high road. The road was the divide of East and West Germany. One side of the road was East, the other side West. As Erich completed his ascent and crossed to the West side of this road, he stopped and turned to face his brother. He gave a big wave and Alfred waved back as tears streamed down his face. The last remaining son in the East, of Gottlieb and Rosalie, quickly got back in his car and drove towards his home in Pessin. On his way he contemplated all that had transpired, with his mind thinking ahead and what he could tell the authorities.

Back home, Margot slept restlessly, wondering how the escape had worked out. This gave her great pains in her stomach as she thought about the safety of her family.

Once Alfred arrived back in Pessin he had a few hours work ahead of him. With the help of his friend, Siegfried, he moved four cows out of his parents' barn. He had previously arranged to stow these cows in another friend's barn. Taking the four cows, tied together in twos, Alfred and Siegfried walked more than an hour on back roads, staying away from any potential interruption to their activity.

The night was turning into early morning of the next day by the time they reached their destination. With the cows settled in the barn, Alfred was dropped off a small distance away from his home by Siegfried, so as to not alert any of the neighbours. Alfred walked home and at 4:30 he crawled into bed next to his wife. Margot, feeling justifiably anxious, and unable to sleep, had been waiting for her husband's safe return and breathed a sigh of relief.

With frayed nerves, Alfred tossed and turned until he finally drifted off. Margot awoke with her children, completed the morning chores and allowed Alfred to snooze later than his usual 6:00 a.m. wake-up time.

Chapter Thirty-three

Alfred Is Questioned by Police

At 7:30 Margot awoke Alfred, exclaiming, "You better hurry and get up. There's lots of activity at your parents' house. Boy, they're going by here fast! The police, the mayor … the leader of the LPG!"

Alfred jumped out of bed and without eating breakfast grabbed his backpack and left abruptly on his motorbike to exit the scene. He began his work route of visiting farmers to perform artificial inseminations. He was relieved to move away from the hub of the area. It gave him more time to think about what he would tell the authorities.

Margot remained at home with her four children and attempted to carry out her normal daily events as best she could. She worried so much, her stomach felt like it contained rocks! To protect her, Alfred purposely did not tell her even one quarter of his actions regarding the escape.

When Alfred arrived home from work late that afternoon, he ate his supper quickly before departing to a neighbour's home just to get away from his property. He knew the authorities would come soon to ask questions and he wanted as much time as possible to think of actions and consequences.

About an hour later, ten-year-old Anneliese arrived on the scene, being sent by her mother to send a message.

"Dad, you have to come home. There is a policeman there. He's waiting to talk to you."

Alfred walked back home. As he approached the waiting officer he searched carefully for the right words of explanation for his family's sudden disappearance. The policeman indicated he would like to speak in private with Alfred, so the pair went into an adjacent room.

"Did you know that your parents wanted to escape?" he demanded.

"No," Alfred answered solemnly choking back tears. The words he had been working on for the past 24 hours were about to be tested. As he tended to be an emotional individual, the tears were very real.

"You know that I am a police helper and so they wouldn't tell me anything."

"I thought so," replied the officer, seeing Alfred distraught.

It was not easy for Alfred to wear two different hats. He had to lie to the police, as he did not want to place himself or his family in great danger. The penalty for knowingly helping another to escape was a prison term. Luckily the officer trusted Alfred's answer and satisfyingly departed.

That same evening, Alfred snuck over to his parents' home after dark. The mayor had locked it up after discovering they had escaped. Alfred knew of a way to break into the house without leaving any signs of forced entry. Once inside he looked for heirlooms and certain other items, including three clear liquor glasses with gold rims (which he still has, to this day). For as long as he could remember those glasses had adorned his parents' china cabinet, now estimated to be over 100 years old.

Four weeks prior to his parents' departure, Alfred had disposed of a pig for his father. The deal had been arranged with a neighbour, Alfred Jeschke, who sold the pig under his own name for Alfred. Jeschke was a member of the LPG.

A few days after the Kienitz escape, Jeschke was summoned to the mayor's office. On his way there, he stopped at Alfred's home for a conversation, as he suspected he knew what the summons was about.

"I will not lie, I will tell them I got it from you," declared Jeschke, "and you do and say whatever you want."

The wheels of Alfred's mind began to turn again as to what story he could use to overcome this difficulty. After considering all the angles he was pleased to come up with one that he thought would make sense.

Sure enough, a few days later, a policeman arrived on Alfred's doorstep, while he was at work. Margot took the message from this officer that he wanted to speak with Alfred about the pig. The policeman requested Alfred's presence at his home in Retzow.

The next morning as Alfred drove to his work appointments, he stopped in Retzow and found the officer in the shade, resting from the seeding of his field. Alfred quietly sat down beside the policeman under the tree, ready for his questions.

"Jeschke said he sold that pig for you but you did not have a pig registered in the mayor's office." (During this chaotic era, all animals in private barns were counted weekly by the mayor's office.)

"Yes, I know," replied Alfred as he began to spin his tale of the circumstances, choosing his words carefully. For the sake of his life and that of his family, he knew, his story needed to sound plausible and convincing to the officer. He must do his best not to stutter! In all his lying glory, Alfred spoke powerfully as his fairy tale unfolded.

"My dad's pig that they wanted to butcher for themselves died about five months ago. My dad came to me and said, 'My pig for butchering died,' so he asked me if I could lend him a pig of my own. That's what I did. My dad said he had another pig, but it was not heavy enough, but he would give it to me later on. When the time came," Alfred carried on, "my dad said 'the pig is heavy enough, you can have the pig now'. So, I wanted to sell the pig on the free market, where I would get the best money for it. But I couldn't do it under my own name 'cause I didn't have my quota on potatoes that I was supposed to have. So I asked Jeschke if he would sell the pig for me. And he did."

The policeman's eyes narrowed as he took a while to digest all that Alfred declared to him. He finally stated, "Yes, that makes sense." Alfred breathed a deep but quiet sigh of relief that his story worked and saved his hide.

Gottlieb and Rosalie's home was locked up; all items were either sold or given away. Remaining livestock was claimed by the LPG. It was a process of months before someone would finally claim the house and move into it.

The authorities were satisfied with Alfred's stories and left him alone. His work in the artificial insemination field proved he was a hard-working citizen trying to earn an honest living. If the LPG only knew …

Chapter Thirty-four

Emil Escapes

In May, just a few weeks later, Alfred's cousin's brother-in-law, Emil, wanted to escape. Alfred knew him quite well and they spoke often during a period of several months before this planned escape.

Alfred borrowed a wagon and horse from Jeschke, drove down to Emil's place and loaded up one of his cows for Alfred to purchase. Alfred drove the cow home, returned the horse and wagon and made plans for the following day, for Emil's big escape. (Emil's wife had left with their son the previous day.)

Alfred picked up Emil during the daylight hours on a Sunday and made the same journey that he had made with his brother Erich, to the border. After parking the car, the pair, with Alfred wearing his cap, walked separately towards the border patrol station, making the authorities think they were strangers to each other. They both showed their passports and crossed over, walked up the stairs to the area where they would walk on West German soil. There, as previously arranged through covert messages, was Alfred's father, Gottlieb, waiting to greet them both. It was an emotional scene of freedom for Emil and a chance for the Kienitz men to see each other again. Out of view from the border patrol, the trio visited for half an hour before Alfred said his goodbyes to the two men. Not wanting to alert the patrol, Alfred placed the cap from his head into his pocket to change his appearance before descending the steps back into East Germany. He showed his passport, then freely came back to his car and drove home. Crossing the border posed a problem mostly when travelling with luggage, and since these men had crossed without any belongings, no suspicion was raised.

On his way back, Alfred remembered that his friend Emil had asked him to go and see Emil's brother, Siegmund, to tell him of the successful escape. Siegmund was married to Alfred's cousin, Elwine. Elwine came joyfully outside when she saw her cousin arrive. Alfred broke the news to her that her brother-in-law and his family had gone to the West. She wept openly, as this was the first she heard about their sudden departure. Emil had not wanted to tell Siegmund of his plans because he knew his brother loved to talk and might inadvertently spoil his escape. Emil relayed to Alfred before his endeavour, "Once you tell Siegmund the news, he can say or do what he wants." That same evening, Siegmund went to Emil's vacated home and removed many belongings before the authorities could get their hands on them. Whenever East Germans escaped, they left most of their belongings behind. If Siegmund did not retrieve items from his brother's house, the authorities would have taken everything.

On his motorbike in July of 1960, Alfred took a trip to West Germany alone. He heard his brother Gustav was visiting from Canada for ten days and paying a visit to his parents, who still lived in West Berlin – as did their daughter, Erna. Alfred and Margot lived just half an hour from the border, so Alfred could visit his family often.

A discussion ensued between Gustav and Alfred about how wonderful a country Canada was. Gustav said he would assist his brother if Alfred was interested in coming to Canada. Gustav said it would not be easy, Alfred would have to work hard in Canada, but he could get ahead if he was willing to do this in the new country. When Gustav mentioned the hunting was excellent, Alfred's ears perked up even more. His thoughts then turned to his young daughter, Anneliese, and his son, Manfred, in grades four and three respectively, and how they had to pull weeds for the LPG during school hours. Hating the Communists and all they stood for, Alfred started to dream of the new country. He was excited to go back home to his wife and express his ideas about a new opportunity.

Alfred made several more day trips to West Berlin in those ten days that Gustav was there. They talked about Canada, about Alfred and Margot going there with their children. They even discussed the possibility of bringing Alfred's beloved hunting dog, Asta, with them.

However, Alfred had a hard time convincing Margot to leave East Germany. She would be leaving her parents and sisters behind, as well as many friends. She was exceedingly close to her mother, as were her children. They spent much time together and Erna, the children's *Oma*, would bake cookies and other goods for them. The children visited their grandparents often. Yet by the time Gustav headed back to Canada, Alfred and Margot had made up their minds to escape to the West and eventually journey to the land of opportunity. Margot was not completely convinced about the whole thing, but she trusted Alfred and his ideas. Alfred was a go-getter and thought this would be an excellent move for his young family.

Summer, 1960 (Reunited on a visit) L - R: Margot, Alfred, Paul (Erna's husband), Erna, Gottlieb, Rosalie, Else, Gustav (Else's husband); in front, Manfred, Anneliese, Wolfgang, Berndt.

Chapter Thirty-five
Alfred Helps in Another Escape

I n early fall of that same year, 1960, Alfred and Margot, her sister Ursula and husband Horst, went out for some evening entertainment. Horst drove, as Alfred had sold his 1936 Opel P4 station wagon (with the intention of escaping some time in the near future). It was late, nearly midnight, when Horst dropped off his in-laws after an evening of fun. Alfred and Margot were getting ready for bed when they were alarmed by a knock at their kitchen window. The young couple did not know that a pair had knocked on their door earlier that evening with no answer, and had waited in the bushes for their return.

Alfred asked who was there.

"Wanke," came the reply. Wanke was a distant relative on Alfred's mother's side, but it took Alfred a few moments to remember this.

Opening the door to a mother who was in her mid-sixties and son who would be roughly thirty, Alfred and Margot invited them in. After some small talk, the Wankes came right to the point. They had heard from secret sources that Alfred had helped others escape and now they were in need of his assistance. The son's passport had been taken away through suspicions of his attempted escape. It would be returned, he was told, in a few weeks' time. What he wanted was to borrow Alfred's passport, as he was afraid the border would be closed soon. Speculation was that this would be a certainty, to prevent more people from escaping. Wanke was so anxious to leave the East that he even offered Alfred thousands of marks for the loan of his passport. After talking for a couple of hours Alfred drew to the conclusion that it was much too dangerous for Wanke to borrow his passport. They would both be placed in jail if caught; the risk was too high. Instead Alfred told the Wankes to wait out their time until the passport was returned, and then come back and he would gladly help them. Although they were disappointed, they thought Alfred's idea was sound.

Mother and son stayed the rest of the night with the Kienitzes. The next morning Alfred took them to a bus station so they could make their journey back home and wait for just the right time to make their escape. He told them to pretend they were Communists, to play the game so the authorities would return the passport and not suspect anything.

Their efforts paid off, for in three weeks the son received his passport back. And, sure enough, they were back on Alfred and Margot's doorstep. Alfred drove mother and son to the border without any possessions. They crossed without any incident. Alfred never heard from them again but assumed they were reunited with their relatives in the West.

Chapter Thirty-six

Siegfried Does Not Take Alfred's Advice

S iegfried Graewe had much in common with Alfred and held similar views. The two developed a strong relationship and were good friends over the years. They found each other trustworthy and helped each other in many ways. The pair dreamed of escaping. Siegfried would want to go to Canada where he had a distant relative in Manitoba; Alfred eventually wanted to join his brother, Gustav in Canada, where he had settled in Toronto.

Siegfried was not so quick with his thinking at times, especially when it came to deceiving the Communists. Thus, when he wanted to escape East Germany he looked to his friend, Alfred, for ideas. Alfred advised him not to have his whole family flee together, but to go separately, so as not to alert the authorities. But Siegfried, with a family of four children and a wife, wanted to keep them together. Alfred wondered: Would it work out for him?

Preparations for departure were extensive. Siegfried's family wore several layers of clothes when making prior trips to the West. They left much of this clothing there, with relatives, to ensure they would have enough to wear once they actually escaped. At home, the closets were almost bare.

Leaving their car in the city of Nauen, the family of six took a train to West Berlin. At a checkpoint, police entered their train car and inspected passports. A man and wife travelling with their four children across the border seemed particularly suspicious to the military officers. After examining their train tickets, which showed the origin of their journey as Nauen, the police confiscated the passports and sent the family back. No argument from Siegfried ensued, as he knew his getaway had come to a grinding halt. The family boarded a train heading east to go back home with heavy hearts, home to their grave disappointment. Had Siegfried taken Alfred's advice, the outcome might have been quite different.

Knowing that the authorities would come to their house to investigate whether this had been an escape attempt, Siegfried was anxious to get back to his car and speed back home.

Once there Siegfried ran to his nieghbour's house (a cousin of Alfred's, named Leo) and asked for an armload of clothes. Leo, a good friend, happily obliged and gave him clothes with hangers to hang in his bare closets. Siegfried rushed home to prepare for unwelcome company.

Sure enough, half an hour after the family arrived back home, the police came knocking on their door to enquire if there was any intention of running off. Seeing that his house was half empty, and not entirely convinced the family was not planning a permanent trip to West Germany, the authorities held onto the confiscated passports for some considerable time.

Alfred did not know that Siegfried's attempt at escaping had failed. When Siegfried came to visit him one day, Alfred was surprised to see him. He told his good friend to pretend to show support for the Communists, to gain their trust in order to recover the passports. Time was running out, though, as hundreds of people fled daily into West Berlin and no one knew *if* or *when* the border would close.

It would be several months before Siegfried and his family would see their passports again. By that time, it was too late ... the border had closed and Siegfried was unable to leave East Germany.

Chapter Thirty-seven

The Great Escape (Their Own) 1961

Siegfried and his family were still living in their East Germany home when Alfred and Margot put into motion their own well-designed plan for leaving.

When helping others flee in the past, Alfred took great caution in all details so the authorities would not get a whiff of what was taking place. His own escape would be no different. He and Margot kept their strategy extremely quiet, not saying a word to their four children, nor discussing plans while they were present. Their plan was in the works for almost a year to make sure all particulars were worked out.

In the days leading up to their escape, Alfred and Margot took turns travelling to West Berlin to deliver concealed items to Alfred's brother Erich, his wife (the other Margot) and twins Klaus and Christiane. Alfred's Margot would bring family teacups and small dishes, posing them as wedding or birthday gifts; she and the children wore extra layers of clothing and left them behind in West Berlin. Alfred also wore extra layers and left them with his sisters. It was more convenient for him, as he could travel alone on this motorcycle and make the complete trip in under four hours.

Cupboards and armoires slowly emptied – so Margot would pile up clothing at the front to make it seem as though they were full, to prevent the children from suspecting anything. Anneliese, seeing the condition of the cupboards one day, hesitantly asked, "Are we going to do the same thing as Klaus and Christiane?"

"What makes you think that?" replied her mother nonchalantly.

"Well, the cupboards are getting empty," Anneliese answered

"No, don't be silly," came the response.

The parents continued to say nothing to their children. They were afraid the children would talk to others at school, and they most certainly did not want the news to spread.

There was a feather duvet that Margot and Alfred intended to transport to the West. They and Margot's mother, Erna, had the duvet spread out on the kitchen floor and were trying to fold it up so it would be small enough to fit in Wolfgang's baby buggy. Suddenly a knock came at the door. As it began to open Margot could see there was a local police officer standing on the other side. Her quick reaction was to slam the door shut. Alfred told her to run in the other room, then allowed the officer to enter. Alfred instantly conjured up a story.

"Sorry, Officer, my wife was undressing; that's why she slammed the door. We are getting ready to bring the duvet to the city to have it cleaned," Alfred fibbed. But he sensed the officer did not completely buy his story. This same officer appeared unexpectedly many times after that, looking for signs that the family was going to take flight, but he was presently unable to snare the Kienitz family in a lie or prove they had plans of leaving the country.

March was the anticipated time when the family would leave. The plans centred around Asta, Alfred's beloved hunting dog, a purebred German wire-haired pointer. When Asta came into heat, Alfred thought it would be no problem, for he carefully calculated when she would give birth and was sure they would be able to take the pregnant bitch to West Berlin when they escaped. But he was wrong – Asta went into labour in March. In Margot's intense words, "We had made all these plans to escape, then it had to be all changed because of the puppies!" (Pictured on cover) The escape was now delayed till May.

The Friday two days before the planned breakout, the local policeman again showed up without warning on his bicycle. Alfred was in the house discussing minor details for Sunday with two cousins, Leo and Ewald, and the roles they would play in the escape. Alfred sported a work backpack to deliver items (three hunting trophies) to Klaus Thiel as soon as the briefing with Leo and Ewald was finished. Alfred hoped that someday Klaus would be able to return these trophies (antlers from three bucks Alfred had shot and butchered). When the policeman popped his head in, Leo and Ewald were completely taken aback and began stammering. Alfred quickly butted in and came up with a cunning cover story.

"Ewald, I'll come check on your cow tomorrow, because I have to go to a meeting right now. You too, Leo, I'll come first thing in the morning," Alfred said, loud enough for the policeman to hear. It sounded like business to the officer (though as Alfred would say, it was really 'monkey business'). Seeing Alfred with his work backpack, the officer soon left so Alfred could be on his way.

Asta finally gave birth to eight puppies, but the law was that only six were allowed to be kept. By the time they were six or seven weeks old the puppies were ready to be sold. Buyers had been lined up for the young wire-haired pups and they were sold for roughly $100 Canadian, a good income for a family about to be on the run. A photo was taken of five of the puppies in their kennel after one of their siblings went to their new home.

The last puppy was picked up on a Saturday, the day before the family was to leave. The buyer gave Alfred a cheque, which presented a huge dilemma, since the banks were closed until Monday. Alfred gave the cheque to a good friend, Klaus Thiel, who would cash it first thing Monday morning, before authorities could catch wind of what was happening. Klaus trusted Alfred completely, so he gave him the money (equivalent to one hundred Canadian dollars) in cash.

Early Sunday morning, Erna Krueger arrived at the Kienitz home to see her daughter and grandchildren off. It was a bittersweet and short visit. Knowing that her daughter and family would have an easier life in another country made the departure a bit easier. Not knowing when she would see them again pulled at her heart and she ached for them all to remain. Margot and Erna were extremely careful not to show too much emotion in front of the children, so as not to give away the plan.

As Margot and the children walked to the bus stop in their town of Pessin, Erna waved endlessly until they were all out of sight. Margot and the children waved until they could no longer see her. Then Margot turned her attention back to the trip ahead of her, Alfred was still at home but would soon leave on his motorbike to deliver more items to Klaus Thiel. Anneliese was beginning to have her doubts about the trip; she had a notion perhaps they were leaving their home for good, but said nothing.

It was too dangerous on this trip to wear any extra clothes or bring household items with them. Margot and the children basically went as if they were going to visit their family in West Berlin for the day. They simply went with nothing that day except the clothes on their back.

Alfred had arranged that his cousin, Erich Kufeld, would meet Margot with Anneliese, Manfred, Berndt and Wolfgang in Nauen at the train station. He would ride along with them in the international train across the border and ensure that the young family arrived in West Berlin without incident.

After Margot and the children descended from the train he would then ride back alone. Alfred knew that Erich should return around noon if everything went smoothly.

After Alfred finished his errands he rode his bike to Erich's house before noon and found his cousin was already home. The plan was working out so far; Margot and the four children had crossed over the border into West Berlin safely. Erich and his wife invited Alfred to stay for lunch, but Alfred felt as if he had a rock in his throat and was unable to eat.

Alfred rode his bike back home and solemnly went into his house for the last time. Turning from room to room, he opened each door and said goodbye to the space that had been occupied by himself and his family for the past ten years.

Walking out of the house with tears welling in his eyes, he greeted Asta at her kennel and opened the door to it. She leapt out with great excitement. Again Alfred hopped on his motorbike with Asta running alongside. Asta was very well trained and quite used to running beside her master. They went along back roads to Siegfried Grawe's house. Siegfried and Alfred loaded the hunting dog into Siegfried's car. Leo then joined them; he and Siegfried rode in the car with Asta and followed Alfred to Nauen. At a gas station Alfred parked his motorbike in an inconspicuous area and rode the rest of the journey in the car with the men and Asta.

They drove to the border at Albrechtshof. The car was parked in an area not detected by the border patrol about 100 metres away. Alfred thanked Leo and Siegfried and said his goodbyes. Alfred had long thought about what he would tell the border patrols so they would allow him to pass through with his dog.

As he had often come for hunting meetings with his dog in the past, this would not seem unusual. Remaining calm and collected was of the utmost importance. At the border, Alfred showed his passport and was not questioned in the least. He walked up the approximately 30 steps to the white line that divided the East from the West. He was taking this path for the *very* last time – the same path that his brothers, sisters and parents had taken before.

After his ascent Alfred turned around to catch sight of Leo and Siegfried. He gave them a big wave as the signal that all was well. His friends returned the wave, wondering what the future held for all of them.

The walk to Alfred's sister's home took about a half an hour. A great sigh of relief was breathed by all when Alfred appeared, the last of the link. Not only were Margot and children there with his two sisters, but also his parents greeted him with open arms. It was an emotional evening to say the least.

The whole Kienitz family had now escaped their East German homes and lives. Alfred wondered what would become of his house and the rest of their belongings. But that was not of major importance; he was just so relieved that he and his family had escaped the Communist country. No one knew if they would ever be allowed back, nor did the Kienitzes know if they would even have the desire to return.

Chapter Thirty-eight

The Displaced Family

The days that followed were very stressful. The first two nights were spent at the house of Alfred's sister (Else). Alfred, Margot and their children now had to register at the refugee camp located on the other side of Berlin. As there were no pets allowed in the camp, and because of personal reasons, arrangements were made the next day for Asta's future. Alfred and Gustav had previously talked about flying Asta to Toronto, Canada. Alfred purchased a kennel and dog food for her flight. The hunting dog needed to be vet-checked with proper papers before boarding the plane; upon arrival she would be quarantined for a period of three months. Gustav would be permitted to visit her during this period and would care for her once she was released. At this time, Gustav was married with one daughter, while his in-laws were residents in the upper level of his High Park, Toronto home. He waited eagerly for word of his brother's safe arrival into West Berlin and for his extended family to join him in Canada.

Once all Asta's care was looked after, the family could concentrate on their dwelling in the camp. The multiple buildings were most likely previously used as an army camp. Flat buildings consisted of rooms with three double beds; each person had his or her own single covers. Couples with no children or just one child would often share a room with another small family. These rooms were filled up to capacity, as Alfred noted that some days between 1,500 and 3,000 people escaped from their former East German homeland. Alfred and Margot were fortunate, as they filled one room completely with their four children, which eliminated the need to bunk with strangers. Showers and bathrooms were shared among all residents and were located on each floor at the end of the hallway.

For the first week the family was required to be out of their room by 7:00 a.m. and stay in a hallway furnished with couches and chairs. During this time rooms were cleaned; most often the family would receive a new room for the next night, sometimes on a different floor. Until all registration was finalized, this turmoil for frightened families and couples continued for about a week. Once all the papers were mainly completed, Alfred and his family were moved into another large four-storey building where they would not have to be shuffled to a new room every night.

A bus came every morning to pick up Alfred and others to take them to various destinations where they would be questioned on anything relating to their knowledge of certain goings-on in East Germany, about the East German Army and anything else that was crucial for the interrogators to know. The refugees were treated very respectfully and fed well during this period. Alfred began to realize that there were certain spies among them, but he and most refugees shared few facts with each other.

The first several weeks were traumatic for the children. Alfred and Margot had planned their escape for some time and worked out details meticulously for their safe journey. They were for the most part prepared. The children, however, had had very little time to digest what was going on. They had left everything behind: their friends, pigeons, guinea hen, toys, bikes, etc. They left their whole life behind! Wolfgang in particular was very sad and cried often that he wanted to go back home. The children missed their grandparents (Margot's parents) terribly.

It was at this time that Margot purchased two large teddy bears for her two youngest boys. The bears were fuzzy and light brown in colour, about 45 centimetres from head to toe. When tipped forward they would release a low 'baa' sound (similar to a lamb, but the pitch much lower) and became much-beloved toys for Berndt and Wolfgang. They still have them to this day!

After ten to fourteen days, with all paperwork complete, the family was moved into a different refugee camp on the outskirts of West Berlin. Here they were housed on the main floor where they could cook for themselves on a very small stove. The one large room was sparsely furnished, but this again would be temporary living quarters.

A few weeks later they were moved out of the refugee camp and were given living quarters by the government. It was a U-shaped two-storey building with all one-room units. This residence would be their home for the next 11 months or so before their trip to Canada. Their new home consisted of a small kitchen area and six single beds. Alfred and Margot pushed their beds together. In one area Manfred and Anneliese slept, in another area Berndt and Wolfgang shared space. Margot sewed curtains and they were hung from the ceiling on a wire.

Alfred had been working since the day all the registration was completed. His first job consisted of putting a galvanized coating on steel. When the family moved to this U-shaped building, he found work in a large factory that employed over a hundred staff working three different shifts making carpets. Both he and Margot had bicycles to ride to their jobs. Alfred started out in a section where he and five or six co-workers took the finished carpet off the machines and folded them to be placed on wagons for various processing.

Margot rode her bike to a garden centre five days a week. There she cut and bundled fresh flowers. Store employees took the flowers to a central station where they would be sold wholesale to flower shop owners. Alfred also worked here part-time, turning soil and doing whatever else needed to be done. The three oldest children attended school, while the youngest, Wolfgang, rode with his mother on her bike to the garden centre and accompanied her while she worked. Margot's boss also had a son close in age to Wolfgang, and they played together. Margot had to keep a close eye on her youngest as he was forever getting into trouble.

After a while Alfred became more comfortable in this workplace and approached his boss to inquire about advancement. The supervisor that he spoke with was a refugee himself, so Alfred could speak easily and openly with him. He explained candidly to his boss that he would like to make more money. He had four children to feed; would it be possible to be placed in an alternative area where he could increase his salary? The compassionate boss, seeing Alfred's dire situation, immediately told him to have no worries, that he would look after him. Alfred was moved shortly thereafter to a new location within the company, in addition to receiving better pay.

In the summer that followed, it was suggested to Alfred and Margot (by Alfred's sisters Else and Erna) that the three oldest children be sent on a holiday. The sisters believed it could benefit them during this stressful time of upheaval. The government had ties with Holland; that would be a good place for the children to go.

Berndt recalled being shipped off to another area of West Germany instead of Holland. Although Berndt was very shy, his entire family, except his mother, thought it would be good for him. His next recollection, from when he was on the verge of turning five, is being on a train and waving profusely to his parents. He was on his way to a sort of children's summer camp. The only memory he has of the camp is sitting in a cafeteria trying to finish his meal. All the other children had eaten and gone out to play, but Berndt sat looking solemnly at his unappetizing spinach. He wasn't allowed outside until he had eaten his entire meal. The burly chef came over, with his apron and hat still on, and struck up a conversation with Berndt sitting opposite to him.

"What's wrong? Aren't you feeling well? Aren't you hungry?" asked the cook in a caring tone.

"I don't like spinach," replied Berndt after some thought.

Warmth was felt between the two strangers after they conversed some more, and the young boy began to eat his cold meal.

Being 'shipped off' was quite a frightening experience for Berndt and it traumatized him for a long time. It was bad enough to have left the comfort of his home and be in a strange city, but then to be separated from his family was quite hard on the youngster. He was quite close to his mother. Margot later regretted sending Berndt away and she could see it had been very troubling for him.

Anneliese's experience was much more pleasant. She left on a train in a pretty dress and sweater early one morning, on her way to a retreat-holiday in Holland. It was arranged by an organization that sent escapee children to various places, to help them cope with their ordeal. Anneliese was placed in a home with a very nice family who had two daughters, both much older than herself. This religious Christian family prayed before supper and made the nine-year-old feel quite welcome. As a parting gift, Anneliese received a small yellow teacup and saucer together with a sugar spoon with Holland written on it. She still has them to this day.

Manfred was also sent to Holland, to a couple in their late fifties. This couple had no children and wanted to experience a child in their home for a few weeks. Manfred recalls a horse-drawn wagon stopping by the home every day, selling fresh meat, bread, cheese, apples and oranges. This was the seven-year-old's first taste of an orange.

Because Wolfgang was very young at the time of the escape from East Germany, his only recollection is of his fright during a lifeboat drill on the ship over to Canada. Everyone was made to wear life jackets in preparation for a disaster, and this extremely terrified the four-year-old.

Chapter Thirty-nine

The Wall

Margot's mother, Erna, came to visit her daughter and family often, as it was not far from her home to travel to West Berlin. She would generally arrive early on a Saturday or Sunday and stay for the whole day. On her arrival, Erna would unpack fresh eggs and freshly-baked cookies for her grandchildren. When it was time for Erna (*Oma* to her grandchildren) to leave, Berndt and Wolfgang expressed a strong desire to go with her. It was a strange situation for them to understand, why they could not visit their grandparents' home. Telephone service was practically absent; there were probably three phones at most in the whole village, so phone communication was out of the question.

One particular Saturday when the children's *Oma* was going to make her weekly visit, the guards confiscated her passport. They gave no valid reason why. They only stated her passport would be returned in two weeks. Without a passport, Erna was unable to cross the border, so she journeyed back home to her husband, Georg, and immediately sat down to write a letter to explain her whereabouts and what had just taken place. Margot and her family were waiting for Erna's arrival; they had no idea why she did not appear. No *Oma*!

On or about the following Wednesday, which was the ninth day of August, *Oma's* letter arrived and gave details to the circumstances of her absence the previous weekend. It explained that she was very nervous and confused. "I just told them I wanted to go visit my daughter. They told me I could go in two weeks." The Kienitzes were very sad and disappointed about this. Alfred and Margot had suspected it would happen sooner rather than later. They surmised the border would be closing someday very soon to prevent the hundreds, sometimes thousands, of refugees that were fleeing East Germany into West Berlin on a daily basis.

Their fears came true.

On Saturday August 12, 1961, at midnight, the border closed up. Families had been separated! Some were waiting for their loved ones to arrive, to be reunited with them. Only those with West German citizenship could visit from West to East. As refugees, Alfred and Margot were not allowed to cross the border. Had they attempted to cross into the East, they would have been jailed.

Alfred and Margot heard on the radio, the following morning, August 13, that the border was closed by placing barbed wire along the walkway.

Alfred heard a story a short while later from one of his co-workers. The names of the people involved in this account have been changed and made fictitious. Bruno's brother, Karl, lived in East Germany with his wife Frieda. Alfred's co-worker Bruno had a son, Hans, who often visited his childless aunt and uncle in East Germany. During the closing of the border, Hans had been visiting with his Onkel Karl and Tante Frieda in East Germany for a period of two weeks when Karl and Frieda wanted to cross the border to return the boy home. It was Saturday, August 12. They were met with resistance and given little explanation why they were not allowed to cross. After advising the border guards that they were returning their nephew to Karl's brother, Bruno, they were questioned at length. After an extensive investigation into their story, the trio was allowed to go across. Spending the night with his brother, Karl and Frieda planned on returning to East Germany the next day. However, when the next day dawned, they, along with the whole world, heard that the border had closed. Karl and Frieda had to face an arduous decision: Stay in West Berlin and leave everything behind, or go back to their home, belongings, and his job as a tractor driver with the LPG. Karl fought in his mind as to what to do. In the end, he and his wife decided to settle in West Berlin and Karl obtained a job at the carpet factory where Bruno worked. The couple left *all* their belongings behind and began a new life.

Chapter Forty

The Reluctance

By the fall, Alfred had been in contact by letters with his brother, Gustav, in Toronto, to begin plans for a crossing to North America. Gustav suggested they come in spring, when jobs would be a little more plentiful and, with the snow gone, it would be easier to get around. At the Canadian embassy Alfred filled out many forms, after which the Kienitz family attended an immigration doctor for examination. All members had a clean bill of health for their prospective journey to the new land.

Hearing that her son had a desire to immigrate to Canada, and being a typical mother, Rosalie tried to talk her son out of leaving. "Why do you want to go so far in the world? You don't know what's going to happen. Don't you have enough bread here? You have so many children; you don't know what's going to happen."

Gottlieb heard his wife shedding tears over her fears of her family being torn apart further. With Gustav gone and raising a family in Canada, Rosalie would be losing another son, daughter-in-law and four grandchildren.

When Alfred was alone with his dad, Gottlieb proclaimed with calmness and sincerity, "Son, if you want to go to Canada, and you think that is the right decision, don't look for us. Just go. We are old, we're going to die away, but you, your future is still ahead of you. If you think it's right, just go."

With his mind made up, Alfred knew there would be tough times ahead in another country away from most of their family. Here they could assist one another, whereas in English-speaking Canada he had only his brother. He did not know what to expect of the strange land, nor what jobs the new country could offer. As well, there would be a language barrier. No one from Alfred's family could speak English!

Alfred was all for leaving Germany. He had read his brother's letters over and over and had become more and more exited about the prospect of a new land. Margot, on the other hand, was not so sure. Although she and Alfred had discussed the prospect of coming to Canada while they were still in East Germany, once they had escaped into West Berlin she had mixed feelings. Living in West Germany was satisfactory to her and she did not want to be even further away from her family, even though at this point, with the border closed, she did not know when she might see her parents or sisters again.

Margot suggested that Alfred should go alone to Canada first, check it out and, if it was really as good as Gustav had said, then she would come too. Alfred said, "No, we all go together or we don't go at all." To which Margot replied, "Okay, we don't go at all."

Alfred argued back, they had to go, there was no other way. No other choice. Margot reluctantly agreed, but her heart was enormously heavy. To leave her beloved parents and sisters, and German-speaking friends and relatives behind was not a welcome prospect.

Rosalie suggested Alfred buy himself a suit before leaving Germany, as she feared money might be a problem in a foreign land. He purchased a suit shortly before his departure.

Chapter Forty-one

More on the Wall

The border in the meantime was undergoing construction of a permanent wall that would further divide East and West Berlin. Houses were demolished and the wall cut through dozens of streets in East Berlin. The construction took months; to accommodate this procedure, a 'dead zone' (also called 'no man's land') was declared between the wall and where civilians would be allowed to be seen. With a total height of 3.65 metres, the wall was 12 centimetres in width at the top and 22 centimetres at the base.

During the formation of the wall, guards patrolled the area. Not only were the border patrols keeping an eye on citizens trying to pass through, they were also watching the workers themselves, as there were fears employees would flee across the border while on the job. Every day the border patrol's shift would alternate. The border guards seldom worked with the same staff on a regular basis, to divert any plans of escaping. When an employee would come to the jobsite and meet others he was unfamiliar with, uncertainty would follow whether his fellow employee could be trusted. This rotation process diverted close relationships; suspicions always arose whether their coworker could be confided in.

Through the grapevine and the news, Alfred heard that when individuals did have ideas of escaping it was with uncertainty. Their friendship and faith would be tested. It would go like this:

First civilian: "Do you want to leave, escape?"

Second civilian: "Do you?"

First Civilian: "I will if you will."

Second civilian: "Well, you go first."

First civilian: "Well, how about we go together?"

Second civilian: "Whoever goes first should take the other one's gun so he can't shoot him as he escapes."

Once on the other side, the pair would shake hands and hug each other, now free men. Only the East side was patrolled by armed guards ready to shoot fleeing citizens; the West was just lightly patrolled. Anyone breaking free to the West would be greeted by a police car which, upon surrender of any guns the escapees might be carrying, would provide a ride to the refugee camp.

After the wall was erected, two double fences about three metres apart and about three metres high were assembled on the East Germany side, on open land. Between the double fences, vicious trained attack dogs patrolled the area day and night. This region was divided into sections where watchdogs would patrol their own small territory. The 'dead zone' was approximately 100 metres wide from the fence to the edge. Civilians could safely venture to the edge, but no further. The area was lit up at night as if it were daytime, for patrol officers to view any suspected activity. Signs were erected to warn those approaching the fences that trespassing was forbidden. Watchtowers, trenches and bunkers were built. There were some areas in which, if any person became visible, that person would be shouted at first, then fired upon if he or she did not retreat. In other patrol areas, anyone spotted was shot without warning. Over one hundred would-be escapees were killed during the Berlin Wall's history

Chapter Forty-two

The Arkadia

Immigration papers having been obtained in the autumn of 1961, arrangements were now under way for the Kienitz trip to Canada. They were to journey on the ship *Arkadia* the following spring. Alfred paid 3,500 West German marks for the six passengers. Dates were given to the family for when they could depart; they chose April 28.

Alfred and Margot got together with relatives quite often during that winter and early spring. On one of their visits to his sister Erna, Erna's father-in-law, whose name was Paul, gave Alfred a delightful surprise. It was a few evenings before the Kienitz departure. Paul, in his 80's, approached Alfred and gave him fifteen marks, declaring, "Some pocket money for you." Alfred was very touched by Paul's generosity!

1961 Last photo of Alfred with his siblings and parents. l - r: Erna, Erich, Rosalie, Luise, Gottlieb, Alfred, Else. Trying to keep their smiles before a sad departing.

One of their last meals with their family…notice the long expression on the adult's faces. l - r: Wolfgang sitting on Else's lap; Oma; Alfred, Anneliese behind Margot; Berndt, Manfred; Opa; Erna

1962 – Alfred, Margot and children spending a few last moments with their rela-tives; sorrow and excitement filled the air. This was in Berlin, prior to departure on their flight from Berlin to Hamburg, from where they would go to Bremen.

An expediting company arrived two days prior to their departure and packed the family's belongings in four large crates for transport to the airport so they could be loaded onto the *Arkadia* ship. The rest of their possessions were packed in three suitcases. After saying their goodbyes the following morning Alfred and Margot and the children flew from Berlin to Hamburg, where they had a stopover before flying on to Bremen. Mixed feelings followed in the days to come, but excitement mostly filled Alfred's heart for the future of his family in a new land.

The stopover in Bremen allowed them a short rest before noon. Rosalie, who was visiting Erich and his wife Margot close by, came alone to meet her son and family. (Erich, also a refugee in West Germany, was saving every penny he earned and could not afford to come with Rosalie.) Rosalie met the young Kienitz family at a pre-arranged location where they ate at a restaurant together.

Alfred, Margot and their children had never before been in a restaurant in the West. Rosalie and the young family of six chose a round table. Sitting on the table were a bowl of pretzels and two other kinds of snacks. As the family was hungry, they began eating the salty munchies while they waited for their orders, presuming that the snacks were complimentary. When the bill came Alfred was astonished to see an extra charge for the snacks! Rosalie quietly paid the bill.

After yet another round of tearful goodbyes the family departed on a train to Bremerhaven, where their ship was docked. A short walk led them directly to the ship. Luck was with them when they boarded the *Arkadia*, as their cabins were discovered to be directly in the middle of the large ship. These cabins were chosen out of regard specifically for their small children. Once out in the ocean, the bow of the ship would rise eleven metres or more before cresting, and then downward motion would send the stern rocking as the ship tumbled into the troughs of the waves. Even with their accommodations in the middle of the ship, the Kienitzes still felt plenty of motion.

April 1962, boarding the Arkadia: Margot with Berndt and Wolfgang. Walking in foreground are Anneliese and Manfred (you can see Anneliese's foot and tailcoat), followed by a tearful Alfred.

One small round window, three bunk beds, and one three-drawer dresser were the main features of their simple lodgings for the ten-day voyage. Upon opening the dresser, Alfred discovered a pair of high-quality binoculars. His excitement soon diminished and he grudgingly surrendered the binoculars to the stewardess when she inquired if they had been found. The previous occupants had left them behind by mistake.

After three days out in the ocean, the ship began its severe rocking motion. The family became seasick along with the majority of the other passengers. Once full, the now nearly-empty dining area demonstrated how the unsettled passengers felt about eating! Alfred still managed to eat, however Margot and the children decided to pass up some of the meals for a few days until they became more attuned to the wave movement. The captain announced later, near the end of the crossing, that in general this passage was rather fortunate, as the waters were moderately calm.

The evening of May 8 marked the *Arkadia's* arrival in Montreal. Retrieving their suitcases and trunks, the family of six joined many others in boarding a train to Toronto. The train passengers were given blankets to cover them while sleeping during the night. Alfred and the children sampled the water from a fountain and instantly decided Canadian drinking water did not taste good – too much chlorine!

The sun was just coming up when the train pulled into the station in Toronto, where they were met by Gustav and his Volkswagen and trailer. They had to make two treks to Gustav's house, the first time with passengers only. Gustav and the newly-arrived immigrants ate breakfast that his wife Anita had prepared, then the two brothers returned to the station to retrieve the baggage. Alfred was overjoyed to see his Asta again; she recognized him immediately, wagging her tail with delight.

The following day the brothers visited the bank so Alfred could exchange his currency for Canadian dollars. Gustav, now ten years in Canada, spoke fluent English and assisted Alfred at the bank. When Alfred converted his money from East to West the currency was 6.50 East mark to 1.00 West mark. This particular Thursday morning the currency was 4.50 West mark to one Canadian dollar. What he ended up with was one hundred and twenty-four dollars Canadian! No table, no chairs, no beds ... no food for his wife and four children. All that they had was what they'd brought from Pessin in four crates and three suitcases. Even with so little money, Alfred and Margot made up their minds that they would *never* give up, they would succeed no matter what it took.

Chapter Forty-three

Canada ... Their New Home

Gustav owned property up north, an 81-hectare (200-acre) farm near Minden that came with an old house and barn. He suggested that Margot could stay at the farm with the four children while Alfred found a job in the city. On weekends, as Alfred had no car yet, Gustav would drive him up to the farm. Gustav promised his brother that, although he himself did not have much money, he would support Alfred and his family any way he could.

For the first trip north, on a Friday evening, seven Kienitzes piled into Gustav's small Volkswagen. Gustav drove while Alfred sat in the front seat with Asta on the floor between his legs and Margot in the back with the four children. They arrived at the farm at around ten o'clock that evening; the house and barn were not visible in the dark and it was extremely quiet, much different from West Berlin and metropolitan Toronto.

They walked into the house, lights were turned on, luggage was brought in and after a few more moments Gustav put his arm around Margot.

"Now, Sister-in-law, how you like this here?" he asked.

"I'm not going to stay here alone," wailed Margot.

The brothers realized right then and there, as Margot broke into tears, that it was a mistake to have come at night, when none of the surroundings could be seen. It was certainly unfamiliar territory for all of them, and for Margot to stay there all alone with four children ranging in age from ten down to only four, knowing no English and having no vehicle ... well, Margot had just come to her breaking point. It was just too much for her to take! Normally a very quiet woman, she just had to speak out about this situation.

The following day, Gustav suggested to Alfred that he stay for a few weeks with his wife, until she felt more comfortable to be there without him. A trip was made to the local grocery store to fetch some supplies and seeds for a garden. Gustav returned to Toronto on Sunday in his Volkswagen, leaving the family to become familiar with their new environment. Alfred ended up staying at the farm with Margot and the children for three weeks, during which time, the family created a large vegetable garden on top of the septic bed.

Alfred then began to travel back from Minden with Gustav on Sunday evenings. At first he stayed with Gustav, his wife Anita (also from Germany), and their one-year-old daughter, Linda, until he found a room to rent in a house. On the first Monday morning that Alfred was back in Toronto, he went with Anita's father to look for a job. Two prospective jobs paid $1.70 per hour, another offered $1.75 per hour. During the interview for that job, which involved boning beef, the Danish boss inquired whether Alfred was experienced and wanted proof of it. He handed a knife and steel flint to his prospective employee and asked him to sharpen the knife. Alfred quickly sharpened the knife and so impressed the supervisor that he was hired on the spot. His weekly income would be $64. He would remain with this employer for almost three years.

The summer up in Minden was hard on Margot. But there were also many good times. She and the children picked wild strawberries; the berries were so small, no one wanted to clean them. But they carried out the tedious job of berry-cleaning, after which Margot baked the bottom for a fruit flan and placed the tiny berries inside. The children were excited to tell their papa when he came up that weekend about the special dessert they helped make.

Every weekend, Gustav and Alfred drove up to Minden, sometimes accompanied by Anita and Linda. Back at the one-room boarding house, Alfred kept his meals simple and often ate supper meals with his brother and family.

At the end of August the Kienitz family moved to Toronto, into an apartment on Dundas Street West. The children were able to begin the school year on time. The apartment was badly in need of fresh paint, so the landlord footed the bill for materials and Alfred gladly painted their new home. It was a noisy area, especially on Monday evenings when the garbage was picked up. The first time Alfred heard the metal containers being knocked around he thought the war was breaking out again.

Margot cleaned various houses and a movie theatre while her children were at school. Her income was enough to pay for groceries. One night a week Alfred attended night school to learn English. Margot picked up the language from the papers that her husband brought home, and from the children once they started attending school.

In the first autumn they were living at this apartment, an ad in the paper caught Gustav's eye. A used Volkswagen was advertised for $750; it sounded like a good deal to him. The brothers checked it out and found it to be in great shape. Alfred and Margot had saved enough money to pay cash for it – and thus the Kienitzes purchased their first vehicle in the new country. Now Alfred had a car – but no driver's licence!

Thinking he had studied enough to pass, Alfred wrote the test at the licensing bureau. With his English still not very good, he wasn't quite sure about some of the questions, so he peeked over the shoulder of someone sitting next to him to get some of the answers. When he handed in his test paper, the examiner took a look at it and gently told him he had one too many wrong, and perhaps he would like to take a second look. Alfred was worried. He figured that the man sitting next to him must have had a different test paper. Having difficulty recognizing which of his answers might be wrong (his reading comprehension was still very poor), he made some corrections and went back to the examiner. With a sympathetic face the examiner told Alfred he had not passed the test. He kindly asked the father of four if he had books to study from, and gave him a few more for his second attempt.

His next attempt at the written test was successful. Shortly after he obtained his beginner's licence, Anita accompanied Alfred for his driving test. Being eloquent with her words, she spoke confidentially to the male diving examiner and asked if he could please speak slowly and clearly to her brother-in-law.

Arriving back after the driving part of the exam, the two men climbed out of the car.

"You got it!" exclaimed the examiner.

"I don't understand what you mean by this," replied Alfred.

When informed that this meant he had passed, Alfred was, of course, delighted.

Living in the city was extremely difficult for the Kienitz family, so naturally they looked forward to their weekends up in Minden at the farm. They would pack up their Volkswagen on Fridays after supper, the four children would pile in the back seat with Alfred and Margot in the front and Asta on the floor between Margot's feet, and off they would go on the two-hour trip to the country. Often Gustav, Anita and Linda would join them.

Chapter Forty-four

And Baby Makes Seven

After remaining at the apartment for almost two years, the family rented a farm in Woodbridge for a few months before moving into a rented house on Darlingside Street in Scarborough. They also traded in their small Volkswagen for a much roomier station wagon

While living on Dundas Street, Alfred worked for a short time with a fellow named Leo, making sausage for his store in Sault Ste. Marie. Leo wanted Alfred to stay and work with him, have his family move up to Sault Ste. Marie and settle there. Alfred was not inclined to make this decision and tried his best to come up with an excuse to stay in Toronto.

He decided that he would spin a yarn about Margot being pregnant and wanting to stay in Toronto, what with having four children and another one on the way. Alfred telephoned Margot and explained the situation that he had to come up with a fib as to why he could not accept Leo's proposal. He wanted to make sure Margot was in on the plan should someone say something to her. His wife agreed, declaring, "Say whatever you want, it doesn't matter."

A couple of weeks later Margot found out she really *was* pregnant!

Neither Alfred nor Margot was happy with the prospect of having another child, another mouth to feed. The young family was struggling financially and had trouble at times paying their bills. It was hard for Margot to accept the situation. The baby was due November 28, on Manfred's birthday.

During this time Margot was not working, as they only had one vehicle. Looking after the household chores and four children kept her very busy. And she became increasingly depressed about the prospects of having another child.

This was something she did not disclose until years later, when the fifth child was in her forties.

In need of more space, the family found a modest home of three bedrooms, and moved into these new rented quarters on October 31, 1964 with a very pregnant Margot. That evening, the four children went out for their first experience of Halloween. They tried to stay together, but Wolfgang became separated from his siblings while running from house to house. When he realized he was lost he went up to one home and told the people there of his dilemma. Having inquired as to his last name, the lady of the house looked in the phone book for Kienitz and found Gustav. Luckily, Gustav and Anita were at home. Gustav told the lady that his brother had just moved in and gave her the address. Wolfgang was driven home by this kind lady. Shortly after the other three children had arrived home from their Halloween outing, Wolfgang arrived as well, safe and sound.

One evening after work, Alfred drove his wife to a doctor's appointment, as Margot did not drive. (It would be Manfred who would teach Margot how to drive in the late 1970s.) Margot began sobbing in the car about their financial situation, and wondered aloud how they were going to afford another child. Alfred told her not to worry, that they would work it out somehow.

"Don't cry; let's just hope it's a girl," he said soothingly. Margot went into labour almost a week overdue. Late in the evening of December 3, a 4.3-kilogram (9 pounds, 6 ounces) girl was born at Toronto's Mount Sinai Hospital. The family was elated about their new pudgy baby sister and daughter, Doris.

As Margot had trouble with varicose veins, the doctors placed stockings on her legs below the knees before the delivery. A couple of days later phlebitis settled in Margot's lower right thigh, just above the knee, causing swelling and immense pain. She was deemed to be in serious condition. So grave was her situation that they tried calling Alfred at work, but were unable to reach him. When he arrived at the hospital that evening, he noticed a volunteer worker sitting outside his wife's private room. As Alfred tried to enter the room, the woman asked him his name.

Upon hearing his answer she told him, "Just a minute, you can't go in there. The doctor wants to talk to you."

Alfred was shaken and wondered what had happened. The doctor was summoned and arrived quickly. As he and Alfred walked down the hallway away from Margot's room, Dr. Kiss gingerly placed his arm around Alfred's shoulder and explained what was happening. Margot had developed a blood clot which had moved through her veins.

"We hope the blood clot will stay in the lung and not travel to the heart," he said. "We have done everything that is in our power. This is now up to somebody else, to have a miracle," he confided. Alfred was shaken!

By this time they had walked back and approached the door to Margot's room. Dr. Kiss advised not to speak too much to Margot and to let her rest, so as to not disturb the blood clot.

Alfred swallowed hard and entered the room. He looked down at his wife, whose eyes were closed. He said a faint hello but there was no response. Alfred stayed only a few minutes before becoming emotional and heading back home to his family, who were excited to hear about their mother and sister. Instead of bringing good news, he told the children how serious the situation was with their mother. Unfortunately, they were not allowed to visit. Margot's condition remained critical for a few days.

As Margot lay in the hospital bed she became very weak, and sensed her grave condition. A turning point came a few days later. As she lay still with her arms underneath the covers she felt someone touch and hold her hand beneath her warm blanket. As she struggled to open her eyes she was astonished to see no one in the room. She later told her family that she believes it was the hand of God; after that experience her condition began to improve.

Christmastime arrived and Alfred did his best to make it a happy one for his children despite the fact their mother was hospitalized. He decided to bring the recipe book to Margot so she could advise him about the marble cake he wanted to make for their brood.

Margot remained in the hospital for almost four weeks. The nurses began joking that pretty soon Doris would be able to *walk* home!

Needing to buy a bathtub for their newborn, Alfred visited the local hardware store. Anita told him the name of the item he needed and wrote it on a piece of paper for him – 'B-A-T-H-T-U-B'. Entering the store, Alfred began to look around to see if he could find the item himself. A clerk approached, asking if he needed assistance. In Alfred's accent and broken English it came out 'Battob'. He repeatedly tried to explain with dimensions and much embarrassment, while his eyes searched the shelves. He became increasingly frustrated. Finally spotting a baby tub on a high shelf above the entrance door, he pointed saying, "Dat ting!"

"Oh, bathtub!" came the reply.

Alfred breathed a great sigh of relief.

The yellow tub was used for many years after the new baby outgrew it, especially when it came strawberry time. The entire Kienitz family would go out picking together, and when it came time to clean the berries they would be placed in the tub before being put into freezer bags.

1965, Darlingside: Doris in her yellow bathtub.

1965, Darlingside; Manfred, Berndt, Wofgang, Anneliese with Doris

Chapter Forty-five

Their First House

In February, the owner of their rented house approached Alfred and Margot and informed them of his intention of selling the house.

"The reason I'm coming to tell you this," the landlord began, "is because you keep the place looking so nice, I just want to be a gentleman to you by letting you know."

The young couple thanked him for his honesty. This development caused the Kienitzes to consider purchasing their own home. They knew that their wallets would have to be tightened up even more. Grocery shopping was a bi-weekly event to save money. No snacks of pop, chips or cookies were ever purchased.

Alfred approached a real estate agent he knew from church, to find out if he could purchase a house with a low down payment. The family's hope was to buy something that needed to be fixed up and was therefore inexpensive. They could not find anything that fit this description. It was a year later when the agent came to the Kienitzes about a house that he thought they would be interested in – a cute one, adorned with three bedrooms, a complete unfinished basement, and lovely backyard in a quiet neighborhood. The address was 79 Rowatson Road in Guildwood Village. The house needed a fresh coat of paint, but otherwise it was perfect. It was listed at $17,900, with $2,000 required as a down payment. The family had managed to put aside $1,500 and borrowed some extra from the bank to cover paint and moving costs. The vendor allowed them to come in and paint, so that when closing time approached the house was considered to be in move-in condition.

April 1 was the moving day. The family required movers and a van to move them into their new home, but being short on money, the parents kept their children home from school that day to help. The movers were scheduled to arrive by 9:30 a.m.; by that time the Kienitz family had their entire household belongings on the front lawn! When the two transporters arrived, the Kienitz family assisted them by handing the furniture and boxes up on the van, while the movers packed their belongings. It was just a ten-minute drive to their new home, where the van backed in and the family assisted the movers with unloading. By 1:00 the movers had finished their task at which time they asked if they could use the phone. Alfred overheard the mover say to his boss, "What do you want us to do now? We're finished. I never moved a three-bedroom house so quick as today!" Alfred, at the age of 35, was very proud of himself and family.

Margot had gone back to work after Doris was born, to help make ends meet. She took a job at Hermann's Meat & Delicatessen and travelled there by bus. Babysitting arrangements were made for her youngest child with a neighbour. Margot eventually noticed marks on Doris's body – presumably caused by her babysitter – so other child care preparations had to be made with yet another neighbour. Quite often one of Doris's siblings would stay home to babysit, most often Berndt.

Margot desired to travel back to East Germany to visit her family. She'd never had a proper farewell, and missed them terribly. By 1968 Alfred and Margot had saved up enough money for Margot and three-year-old Doris to travel to Germany for a visit. It was the first time that Doris met her grandparents and German relatives. Margot kept a low profile in the beginning while there, as her visa had not come through until after she arrived in her native land.

A couple of years later Margot received a telegram from her younger sister. It explained that their mother had passed away and was already buried! Margot was devastated, as were the children, especially Anneliese and Doris. Such a shock it was to Margot … That was the last time that Doris ever saw her mother cry.

The four eldest children all decided to change their names while living in Toronto, to reflect their Canadian existence. They would now be known as Anne, Fred, (although Fred went back to Manfred years later) Bert and Wayne.

Alfred continued his love of hunting and often went with his brother or friends to northern Ontario or Manitoba. One year Alfred went moose hunting with a group of three other men. They had four tags altogether and managed to get their quota … but it was Alfred who shot all four moose. Doris still recalls the distinct strong wild smell of the hanging moose in their Rowatson Road garage that fall.

Shortly after the Kienitzes moved in to their new home, Anne met Ray Pronovich, whom she married. The newlyweds moved north to the Bancroft area, where they still live today, as do their daughter, son and four grandchildren.

Around 1970 Margot began working for another meat and delicatessen shop called Bittner's.

Erna, Georg Krueger, celebrating an anniversary

Rosalie, Gottlieb Kienitz - celebrating their 50th wedding anniversary

1970, in Toronto

Chapter Forty-six

The Butcher Business

While working with Heinrich Mayer at Vienna Meats, Alfred was approached by his fellow employee one day about a business that was for sale. Heinrich had a farmer stand at the St. Lawrence Market in Toronto, on the corner of Front and Jarvis Streets, selling fresh meat and sausage every Saturday. News travelled to Heinrich of a butcher business that was for sale in Hagersville, Ontario, a small town 45 kilometres south of Hamilton. A stand at the St. Lawrence Market every Saturday was included in this deal.

"You should buy the butcher business, you're a butcher, your wife is a butcher, it could be a good business for you," he advised Alfred.

Having never heard of Hagersville before, Alfred decided to pay a visit to the market one Saturday to talk to the owner of the meat stand that was for sale. After viewing the 7.7-hectare (19-acre) property in Hagersville with Margot a short while later, he decided to buy the business, which included a farm as well as the farm stand at the market. The seller of the Hagersville business eventually started calling Alfred 'Fred' and the name stuck.

In November of 1971, Alfred and Margot moved their three teenaged boys and young daughter to the small town that bordered the Indian Line. Their new business would be called 'Fred's Meat Products'. Before taking over the business, Margot asked the former owners how much money they should bring to the market for a float. They informed her she would need one hundred and fifty dollars. Margot gasped! They didn't have that kind of money! Putting all their savings into the down payment left them with little cash. After the Kienitz family moved to Hagersville they luckily had a few custom meat orders. Some of the customers paid cash ... now they had their float for the market.

"The Lord works in mysterious ways," remarked Alfred.

The St. Lawrence Market was a busy place and Alfred and Margot made quite a reputation for themselves selling quality meats.

Alfred, Margot and Manfred slept Friday evenings for a few hours before their alarm woke them up at 10:30 p.m. After loading the truck they would arrive at the market by 1:30 a.m. to unload. Customers, mostly Asians, began to arrive after closing their restaurants in the late evening. As their business grew, Alfred counted as many as 35 customers who would be waiting for them when they arrived at the market to begin their busy period. Most likely by ten o'clock every Saturday morning the Kienitz family would be sold out and would pack up for the long hour-and-a-half drive back to Hagersville. After unloading at home again and getting a bite to eat, they were ready for a lengthy nap.

Driving home from their very first market, Alfred and Margot knew they had done well. Margot counted the money as her husband drove. With amazement and delight she counted aloud, proclaiming how much money they had made. It was quite the excitement and they knew then they had made the right decision.

Alfred worked extremely hard, practically seven days a week, visiting auction sales, butchering, cutting, wrapping and attending the market. Margot worked just as hard helping with the business and looking after the household chores. Eventually, Wayne began working with his parents, and took over the business when they retired.

Chapter Forty-seven

Off to Cheapside

Alfred and Margot kept up the heavy pace with 'Fred's Meat Products' for ten years before Alfred decided it was too hard on his nerves and body. They had managed to save enough money to become semi-retired in the small community of Cheapside (population approximately 75). They moved there in 1982 with sixteen-year-old Doris, to a 40-hectare (100- acre) farm, where they began to raise sheep, cattle and hay crops. (Bert and wife, Heather and three children as well as Manfred were now living in Alberta.)

The couple had many happy years on this farm. Margot enjoyed tending to her chickens, crafting, and playing hostess to their many family and friends. Alfred kept busy with the farm animals and continued to hunt.

Margot's health began to diminish rapidly. After two surgeries close together in the fall of 2005, one on her knee and the other to replace the battery in her pace maker, she was put on oxygen at home.

On the morning of Saturday, January 21, 2006, Doris came over early to help her mom shower. It was a humbling experience for both of them; Margot had once looked after Doris, changing her diaper, now Doris was assisting her mother in the shower. Once Margot stepped out of the tub Doris reinserted her oxygen tube, got her mother settled and left for her home just around the corner. Margot later warmed up some homemade soup she had made the day before for herself and Alfred to eat their *Mittagessen* (it was lunchtime, but for them it was their supper and main meal of the day).). The pair sat down just as on every day, and prayed before they ate. Margot, who had periodically choked on food and liquid over the years, began choking from the soup. She gasped only once for air before collapsing. Alfred called 911 and was so distraught, he couldn't find the words to speak. The female operator handed the call over to a male dispatcher who only asked him questions to which he had to answer yes or no, the first question being, "Do you live at RR#2 Nanticoke?" Alfred replied in the affirmative. The operator then gave him details of how to perform CPR. Once the fire department arrived Alfred called over to Doris's house to inform her of the circumstances. Paramedics were the first to arrive on the scene ... Alfred knew it was not good. After being taken to the hospital Margot was hooked up to a breathing apparatus. The doctor advised the Kienitz family that Margot's lungs 'were shot' ... there was nothing they could do for her. With no available beds in the area, Margot was transferred to a Kitchener hospital. After several difficult phone calls to other family members, Doris, Alfred and family headed to Kitchener with the grim realization that they were losing a beloved wife and mother. Bert, Heather and Manfred got on the next plane to Ontario and by midnight all of Margot's children and most of her grandchildren had surrounded her bedside. With medical experts unable to fix her weak lungs, she passed away around noon the following day surrounded by her loving family. After being married for fifty-three years and enduring many hardships, Alfred quietly kissed his wife's forehead with tears saying, "Till we meet again, Margot."

Alfred, in his 80's, still lives in the same home in Cheapside and continues to drive his quad back to the bush every day to observe the wildlife. He was still out in the field cutting/raking/baling hay until he was 78! He now rents out his farmland to his son-in-law, John Sheppard, for soybeans and wheat. His grandson, Alex, (Doris's middle child, aged 22), has a basement apartment in Alfred's home. The two keep a close loving eye on each other.

Children of Rosalie and Gottlieb

Erna (July 21, 1913 – December 12, 2000);
Else (November 18, 1916 – May 30, 2005);
Siegfried (September 9, 1920 – December 3, 1941);
Erich (b. May 18, 1925);
Gustav (b. February 27, 1928).
Alfred (b. January 2, 1930);
Luise (Liesel) (b. May 15, 1934)

Acknowledgements

This book has been five loving years in the making. I actually began writing this in 2005 when my mother was still alive. After taking a long break I was unable to locate the disc with all the saved information. Luckily we hadn't written many pages. Dad and I resumed in 2007 and shared many tears together, some of them happy but many of them sad tears. I want to thank *you*, Dad, for your stories told to the best of your knowledge … for sharing all these great memories. Thanks to Mom & Dad for teaching us children so many important things, for all your love and support, and for taking a chance on coming to a foreign land which is now our *home*.

I thank my amazing husband, John, for his love and support; my fabulous kids: Michelle (for her help in choosing a title), Alex (for helping to look after *Opa*) & Philipp (for doing some editing); wonderful step kids; great in-laws Stan & Mary; super supportive friends Sharon Motley, Darlene Dubniczky & Audrey O'Marra; divine Yoga students (you teach me too!); amusing and spiritual friends-Kim, Terri and Janet; Karen V., Loretta M., Mary G., Heather B., Cheryl M., Nancy F., Tanya S.; Gary Weber (you are awesome!); Ryan Davidson (you too!); Stan of the Port Dover Maple Leaf (you were a great boss who took a chance on my writing skills, many thanks for that break!); Jerri Whiting (awesome shots!); my editor George Downs of The Corporate Word; thanks for filling in some blanks and looking after me when I was little: Anne, Manfred, Bert & Wayne; thanks for filling in more blanks: *Onkel* Erich, *Onkel* Gus, *Tante* Anita, *Tante* Liesel, *Onkel* Ulf, *Tante* Ilse, and Regina; Ray; Heather; mom, who never got to see it, as well as Gwen. So many of you have touched my life in countless ways. Thank you, thank you, much love to you and bless you all! Many Oooomms

Alfred Kienitz, 81 years old, Cheapside, Ontario, Canada, July 2011
[Photo by Doris Kienitz]

About the Author's Family

Anne and Ray Pronovich live near Bancroft, Ontario. Their daughter, Amy and husband have three sons; son Joey has one daughter. Manfred never married and lives down the street from our brother Bert in Millet, Alberta. Bert and Heather have three children: twin daughters Lisa and Leanne and younger brother Mike. Lisa and her husband have a daughter and son; Leanne and her husband have a daughter. Mike is single. Wayne lives in Hagersville, Ontario; he has a daughter, Jessica.

Alfred and Margot's journey to Canada proved to be adventurous and lucrative; they created a bright future for their children with many an opportunity awaiting them. Alfred and Margot produced nine grandchildren. In the fourth-generation lineage, there are seven great-grandchildren ... with more to come, I'm sure.

Doris Kienitz, July 2011
[Photo by Jerri Whiting]

What 'If'
Upon arrival, give a warm hello
When you depart, a heartfelt farewell
Make everyone you meet feel special
Most will be receptive
Some may not
For you never know
'If' you shall ever meet their company again

*~ **Doris Kienitz***

About the Author

Doris Kienitz lives with her husband John Sheppard on the outskirts of Selkirk, Ontario on a farm with their dogs and cats. Together, they have seven children: Michelle, Alex & Philipp; Melissa, Sarah, Amanda and Steven and 2 grandchildren, Kirby and Charlotte. She cherishes her whole family and all her amazing friends. Her love of writing developed as a teenager, writing songs and poems; she wrote for a local newspaper as a single mom in her thirties. In 2008 Doris quit her stressful fulltime position as a Rural Route Mail Carrier to teach more of her passion: Yoga. Teaching since 2003, she loves to share the benefits and appreciates the oneness of life. Doris believes everything happens for a reason. You learn one way or another from your mistakes. For every cause there is an effect, for every action, a reaction. So many circumstances led her parents to flee East Germany and then to the new country of Canada, to make a better life for themselves and their children and for generations to come. There are so many 'what ifs' in life and to think that 'if' her parents had taken a different path in many situations…life would have been so much different! "Thanks, Mom & Dad! From all of us! Love you lots!"